RUNES FOR T.

RUNES FOR TRANSFORMATION

USING ANCIENT SYMBOLS
TO CHANGE YOUR LIFE

KAEDRICH OLSEN

WEISER BOOKS
San Francisco, CA / Newburyport, MA

Hail to the Whisperers

First published in 2008 by
Red Wheel/Weiser, LLC
With offices at:
500 Third Street, Suite 230
San Francisco, CA 94107
www.redwheelweiser.com

ISBN: 978-1-57863-425-5
Library of Congress Cataloging-in-Publication Data is available on request.

Cover design by Maija Tollefson
Text design by Kathryn Sky-Peck
Typeset in Sabon
Cover photograph © Peter Zelei/istockPhoto.com

Printed in Canada
TCP
10 9 8 7 6 5 4 3 2 1

The paper used in this publication meets the minimum requirements of the
American National Standard for Information Sciences—Permanence of Paper
for Printed Library Materials Z39.48-1992 (R1997).

CONTENTS

INTRODUCTION

These days, as you peruse the stores for books on runes, you may notice the titles all fall into two major categories. The first covers the purely educational texts used in collegiate studies. These scholarly books, written by people who worked to get their advanced degrees in Germanic and Scandinavian studies, are very good sources on the historical and literary uses of runes.

The other type of rune books can be found in the New Age section. These books have a portion dedicated to the scholarly study of the runes, then they tend to focus heavily on the divinatory use of runes. Runes, used as a spiritual tool, are excellent for divination. I have used them in this capacity since the mid-1980s, and I have developed my own style of runic divination, as have many others. Divination is all part of the foundation for the recovery of rune wisdom. There are also a few rune books that excel in providing information outside of the divination spectrum; they cover such aspects as runic magic and shamanic arts.

It is good that we have this range of material available today. It means that a great foundation has been laid for the full recovery of the wisdom of the runes.

In Northern Europe, runes were used for many purposes. Their primary purpose was for written communication, and in this capacity, they have been taken nearly all over the world. Outside of communication, runes were mainly used as transformative tools. This transformation could be anything from healing to victory in battle. Although rune literature contains only scant few and vague references to the divinatory use of runes, there are numerous references to the runes being used for transformation purposes.

This wisdom was passed down to us through the ages within the very words and values we use today. The modern English language today is a distant relative of the runic language spoken over a thousand years ago. The people who spoke this language lived in the lands of Iceland, Norway, Sweden, and Denmark, and many of the beliefs, customs, and ideologies that they used are still alive and well within us today.

Runes are a sacred alphabet similar to Sanskrit and Hebrew. Although many of the ancient Norse techniques for using runes did not pass down to us, we can effectively compare them to the practices found in these other spiritual language systems. For example, sacred Hebrew songs, Hindu mantras, and rune songs all have very similar functions. In fact, I believe that a deep study of the runes and their history would not be complete without a comparative analysis to the Hindu, Tibetan, and Jewish beliefs and practices. All of these individual cultures seem to have come from a common root. Even though they use different words and have varying techniques, the messages and results are the same. This congruity is an indication, to me, that humanity does indeed stem from a single source. There must be some sort of a root that can be tapped into for the transformative effect. The subsequent processes are the results of various languages and cultures translating that root into forms they easily understand.

A Brief Note on Translations

I do not claim to be an expert on ancient Scandinavian languages. I have had no formal training on the subject. But through my years of studying the runes and the ancient lore, I have amassed a fair amount of knowledge of Old Norse language. For this reason, I feel comfortable in presenting my own translations.

In this book you will find various passages from *The Poetic Edda* and *The Prose Edda*. It is with the diligent efforts of the experts that I was able to achieve my translations. I tip my hat to Richard Cleasby and Gudbrand Vigfusson for their *Icelandic-English Dictionary of Old Icelandic* and to Geir T. Zoëga for his

Concise Dictionary of Old Norse. These books helped me to fill in the gaps I faced with the language.

In the section to come on runes, I refer to three ancient rune poems. This is to offer the different perspectives the ancients had to the same runic energy. The translations of these poems are not my efforts. Rather, I deferred to Bruce Dickins's great work of 1915, *Runic and Heroic Poems of the Old Teutonic Peoples.* The rune poems presented are taken from this book.

Runic Techniques for Transformation

The time has come to bring the deeper workings of runes into the modern world. It is time to update the transformative processes and make them accessible to a greater number of people. This book is the first step in that direction.

Since I was sixteen years old, I have studied the runes. I have delved deep into the lore, history, and evolution of the rune. Part of my understanding of the runes came from the teachings of the Rune Guild. I also have had many years of successfully reading and teaching runes in a professional capacity, and a fair amount of this time was spent teaching their transformative effects. From these experiences, I have developed effective systems and processes for working with runic energies. These techniques have produced dramatically powerful results. In fact, many of the techniques that I teach helped me to put this book together. I used them to open myself to receive inspiration. The runes helped me to find the right words and maintain a solid flow of these words. It was the runes that lead me to find Red Wheel/Weiser to publish with.

What you will find in this book is an amalgam of ancient runic wisdom and modern transformative techniques, including hypnotherapy, affirmations, neurolinguistic programming (NLP), visualizations, and meditation. (The book also includes a bit of sociology, so you can understand the social perceptions involved with the collective unconscious.) These techniques are what I have learned and taught as I ran a transpersonal hypnotherapy practice. We will explore just a few of them and how they directly apply to rune wisdom.

Not all of the techniques are authentic or historically accurate. There are a lot of holes in the literature on the practice of runes, partially due to the ravages of time and partially due to the coming of Christianity and its attempts to stamp out the practices. In order to make all of these techniques effective, some of these historical holes are filled in with comparative techniques from other traditions. The remaining holes were filled in with my own personal experiences. I see no problem with applying my own work to the runes, because everything that is written down and taken as doctrine by any religion or spiritual system was once someone's personal gnosis.

Within the work that I do, there is a vast body of theory, but I cannot claim to be the origin of it. I work with a group of spiritual beings I choose to call the Whisperers. They have been with me my entire life, guiding me through many situations and giving me a great deal of teachings. It took me years to document the theories that the Whisperers gave to me. Then it took me quite a bit of time to synthesize this theory into working practice. Once I knew that I had the proper techniques, they had to be tested. I taught friends and relatives these powerful runic practices, and they were astounded by the results. I then completed my studies in hypnotherapy and counseling and was able to turn these runic techniques into a practice.

Creating Your New Life

Commitment and Belief

Using the transformative techniques in this book requires only two things:

1. **Commitment to change.** If you approach these techniques half-heartedly, they will not work.

2. **Belief that you can change.** If you have the attitude of "I'll believe it when I see it," nothing will work for you. You must dive into your transformation with both feet. It is not the belief in the system that

you need, rather the belief that you can make the change. This belief in yourself comes when you make the full commitment to change.

This process for change is self-perpetuating and has a cumulative effect. The more you do it, the stronger your power becomes until your transformation is unstoppable. In fact, the stronger your motivation to change, the quicker that change will come.

An easy but powerful first step to take in making this commitment is to make a list of motivators. The first thing I ask you to do is take stock of yourself and find out what moves you. Ask yourself why you want to make this change. Is it for a better life? Do you want to be there for your children when they grow up? Do you want to make a change in the world? Some of the best motivating factors you have are the small things—the small things that add up to make life more worthwhile. But if your motivating factors are huge, then more power to you.

Once you have your list, keep it someplace where you can see it and be reminded of just why you want to make this change.

Stepping-stones

The work that you are about to embark upon is not daunting, but it will inevitably change the world that you live in. For this new world to be stable, it must be created with simple little baby steps. Any drastic change will be unstable or traumatic. Both are situations that will ultimately not be beneficial to any goals you have set for yourself.

If your new reality is unstable, you will find yourself back in the same rut you were in before. In fact, you may be deeper in it, and you will face a new doubt—a doubt that you can change. You may even develop new blocks to reaching your goal. A change in a person's life is actually a death—the death of the old you and preparation of the new you. If there is no chance to reconcile, reassure, and possibly forgive your old self, the transformed self will be no different than a repression of your old self. When there is repression, there is always a reemergence. For this reason, transformation in small steps is required. Ultimately, the purpose of taking it slow is so you can plan out and prepare yourself for your new life.

For your first time using the processes in this book, do not choose anything life-changing or dramatic. Keep the transformation small and simple. Doing so will build your confidence in your ability to change. Once you understand how this process works and how you fit into it, you will find it easy to move on to bigger achievements. For now, keep the working to minor issues that will affect you only in the temporary moment. Some suggestions are to use them when job seeking, to improve your success in something you are already working on, or to improve or restart your love life.

The most important thing that working with the techniques in this book does is change attitudes. With this process, you will be able to see little effects as you change the words you speak and think with. These changes are subtle but effective. Altering the word patterns you have grown accustomed to will begin to change the way your subconscious mind processes your reality. With this simple change, many things in the conscious reality will also change.

Remember, the route to every major goal is nothing but a series of small steps. Many of these steps are backwards, to the side, or around or over some obstacle. As long as the steps are being taken, you are always in pursuit of your dreams. When you stop moving, the goal will not be achievable. There is only one rule about the speed you go to achieving your goal: go at a pace that makes you begin to feel uncomfortable, but never any faster. Change is supposed to be strange and new. If you are comfortable and at peace with your progress, then you must step up your pace a notch. Allow yourself to move out of your comfort zone and be on edge. This is where the real magic happens.

While you are taking baby steps, you must always be in contact with your self. Because you may be in a state of slight disruption with the changes you are making, self-care is rule number one.

Overcoming Setbacks and Blocks

Be prepared for setbacks and failures. No road to success is completely straight and narrow. It is always fraught with obstacles and objections. It is how you learn from these delays that will ensure the stability of your future world. But if there is any sort of setback, it will be small and easy to recover from. These little setbacks only come with taking little steps toward the achievement of your goal. Setbacks are part of the normal process of growth and change.

As you approach your goals, things may come up from your past or present. Issues that you thought were put to rest may resurface. They will present themselves as blocks. These blocks might come in the form of the voice of someone in your past telling you that you cannot succeed or in the form of an overwhelming emotion that freezes you, for example. They may even manifest as actions of self-sabotage. When you encounter a setback, you may face a sense of defeat. You may feel that the roadblock is insurmountable.

There are two ways to overcome blocks. The first is to go back to the drawing board. In essence, take a break and analyze what happened. Reassess the road and find a way around the blockage. The second is to understand the blockage and release it.

For example, let's say Jenny is trying to lose weight, and she just cannot break the 200-pound mark. She needs to reassess her eating plan, exercise patterns, and any other behavior patterns. Getting around her roadblock may be as simple as changing the way she eats or increasing the amount of exercise she gets. Releasing roadblocks takes some self-analysis and self-honesty. For everyone, in any situation, the pitfalls will differ. These types of setbacks are not a sign of failure or even that something is wrong. This is a part we all have that may be in need of attention, reaching out to communicate. As we have all progressed throughout our lives, we have learned certain behaviors from the situations we have encountered. Our psyches are designed to protect us. They want to preserve the core of our being, the essence of our nature. They do so by creating behaviors and beliefs that are beneficial in times of stressful and traumatic situations. As we grow older and are no longer in those stressful or traumatic situations, these patterns now become roadblocks.

If changing her routine does not work, perhaps there is some self-sabotaging happening. Perhaps she notices that every day after work she engages in binge eating, thus counteracting her exercise and healthy eating. Now she must determine why she is doing so. Let's say her work has been extra stressful recently, and she realizes that when she encounters stress, she soothes herself with food. To counteract this action, she might just need to learn healthy techniques to release stress. Once she is able to let go of the stress, she may find that breaking the 200-pound barrier is now easy. All it took was a moment to check in and find out what was going on.

Negative beliefs about authority and a sense of nondeservedness are two major roadblocks that many people face. For many, these particular blocks may have resulted from disciplinary events at school or home. They may even be traced back to moments of abuse. At the time the initial events were happening, these beliefs or behaviors served to protect. They allowed us to move on and live another day.

For example, as you encounter a stressful situation with an employer, you may revert back to a behavior from childhood. This behavior may result in subservience, retraction, or even passive-aggressiveness.

For example, John was trying to get a promotion at work but seemed to miss it every time. As he stepped back and reevaluated the situation, he was reminded of past events, in particular one that happened in childhood. At age five, he was given the task of taking out the garbage. The trash cans were large and usually full, and often the trash would fall out of the bags onto the floor. John's father tended to overreact when this happened and would spank John for making a mess.

Then, when John was a teenager, he got a job as a cook at a local fast-food chain. He was also expected to work long hours cleaning. No matter what John did, or how long he worked, John's boss was never satisfied with the job John did.

Little did John know but both of these experiences planted a belief deep within his subconscious that authority figures were unkind and demanding. In addition, he came to believe that he could not do a good job at anything he did. These beliefs were still at work, albeit unconsciously, at his current place of employment. His performance reviews, attendance, and attitude would worsen every time he learned that he was being considered for a promotion.

What could John do about his situation? Perhaps something as simple as acknowledging the behavior and making a conscious effort to change it. He might need help from a counselor to better understand and resolve these old issues. What must be understood is that carrying this message was not a failing on John's part. It was simply a part of his being, and it was now raising its hand and saying, "Hey, pay attention to me."

By reframing his beliefs on authority and self-deservedness, John was able to make the necessary changes in his life. Where he once saw authority figures as demanding tyrants, he began to see himself as a coach sharing his understanding. Where he felt he would fail if he attempted anything new, he came to see new situations as roads to learning. Roads on which mistakes were seen as an opportunity for learning.

A setback or anything that gets in your way of reaching your goal is really a part of you, not a sign of failure or even that something is wrong. It is a part of you in need of attention and is reaching out to communicate. A block is simply a part of your being that has come from your past, raising its hand and saying, "Hey, pay attention to me." It is also a part of your being that believes it has been providing some sort of service to you. To simply dispatch it and be rid of it would dishonor your past and all that has lead you to this point. It is the behavior that must change, not any part of you or your past. In the case of the person self-sabotaging her efforts to lose weight, she needed to self-soothe. Her roadblock was the fact that she was dealing with her stress in a way that worked against her efforts to reach her goal instead of supporting it. When she realized that, she took a moment out of her day to release her stress. She let go of her job, her title, her duties, and her responsibilities. For just an hour a day, she became a child again. She played, danced, and sang. These activities released her tension and brought her back to a sense of happiness. For her, the part calling for attention was an inner child in need of self-nurturing. If she were to abandon that part of her being, then she would have had a hole that she might never have been able to fill.

Stopping or quitting the pursuit of your goal in the face of a block is an option only in certain cases. If you determine that the rewards of your goal are outweighed by the costs involved, then it is reasonable to stop. You may also choose to stop if your goal no longer exists. For example, if your goal was a promotion at work, and someone else got it, the prize is no longer there. In this case, you may choose to find another goal or achieve a similar goal with another company.

When setbacks happen, take a moment to take a breath. Do not push yourself. You must deal with the stuff that has presented itself. Face your internal issue with compassion, understanding, forgiveness, and honest curiosity, and it will actually tell you how to it needs to be resolved. A therapist or counselor may help you to unravel this internal mystery. Do not hesitate to consult a professional if you find yourself stuck or facing an internal dilemma that is beyond your ability to resolve on you own.

Adjunctive Therapy

While we have been discussing the use of this book's practices as being successful with only minor issues, it can and does work with major ones as well. However, this process is not the be-all and end-all. Not all processes work for every situation or with everyone. Some issues may need more than one process to be overcome. For this reason, if you are facing a major issue, the work in this book must not be the primary process.

If you are dealing with major issues such as addiction, physical illness, or trauma release, you must work with a professional. If you have a disease and want therapy, you must see a doctor. If you are encountering a great deal of sadness or grief, you must work with a trained counselor.

When you seek professional guidance, you must let the counselor know about the work you are doing with this book as well. This knowledge will help them understand the progress you are making, see why roadblocks may suddenly set up, and make necessary treatment plans.

$$\left(1\right)$$

THE NATURE OF REALITY
AND HOW TO CHANGE IT

Today there is a common perception that we are separate from and at the mercy of the reality around us. This is not so; we are our own reality. Many of the great spiritual systems of the world work to help us achieve two goals: they seek to connect us with the world around us and to free us from the illusion that we are separate from it.

Not only are you a part of the world around you, but in a very real sense, you also *are* the world around you. To complicate matters even more, so is everyone else in your world.

Are You "You"?

To focus on this principle, we will look at two aspects of you: you and You. The you is where your perception of self resides—that is, for want of a better word, your ego. Your name, occupation, body image, place in society—all of these things make up the you. This is where the perception of self ends for most people.

Also associated with you is You. This You is all of the elements in the world about you. This is not your occupation, but where you work and whom you work with. The You is also the house you live in, the car you drive, the town you live in, your friends and family. All of these things in "your world" are really a greater aspect of yourself. These are people, places, and things drawn to you and to which you are drawn. All of these aspects are deeply connected together by a higher state of your being.

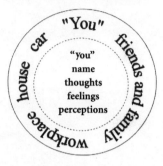

The you and You connection

This connectedness is difficult to perceive. There are many common roads and explanations for the origins of this universe we live. What seems to be evident is that we may all be part of a great experiment, but the details and purpose of this experiment are not clear yet. It is also evident that we all exist, as a whole, in a world that cannot be logically disproven. Conversely, the spiritual world, as we know it, cannot currently be logically proven.

Another aspect of our universe is the fact that we exist in a commonly agreed upon reality. This level of being is in conjunction with the You level of existence. In this world, we have all agreed upon a certain set of rules. While not readily evident, these unwritten rules exist at the collective unconscious level. These rules include gravity, laws of physics, and natural law. When we see a table, we all agree it is a table and agree to its physical properties. We cannot move through it; it has weight, texture, and color. We may not always agree upon its function, but we agree that it exists and on how it exists.

This commonly agreed upon reality is where all of our individual universes overlap. It gives us room to play around and experiment with all of the neat little things in our own personal universes. Where your You exists, so do the other Yous of other people. We call this "interaction." These interactions remind us of who we are at the you level. Take a look at all of the elements in your life. What are they, who are they, where are they? What do they all have in common, besides you? If you look long enough, patterns will emerge and start to make sense. Keep an open mind.

These patterns come from a simple universal principle: similarities attract and perpetuate. This principle means what you are you draw onto you. How you live your life is how your life is. Those people in your You world are simply reflections of you. If you guessed that You is a direct reflection of your you, you would be right! Tied in with that principle is the notion of spiritual attachment. It is an integral function of the evolution of the human soul that like minds be drawn together and attach to one another. If we were to witness this process from a faraway view, it would seem as if we were watching a great wave of minds, a wave that ebbs and flows outside of the effects of time and space. This wave exists in the medium of the collective unconscious.

Layers of Reality

The nature of reality presented so far is just the beginning of the layers of reality. These layers intermingle and intertwine. Quite often they are indistinguishable, but they are always there. I define these levels of reality as subjective, objective, spiritual, and Ginnic realities.

Subjective Reality

Subjective reality is the combination of you and You. This is the reality you perceive with all of your senses; you can think of it as your perceived reality. This level of reality is created by who you are and your growing understanding of the world around you. This level of reality is not exclusively yours. As we interact and mingle with other realities, other people's perceptions become ours as well. Can you think of a time when your understanding of something was changed by someone sharing his or her ideas? Other people's views of reality are often all that we need to change our subjective reality.

Objective Reality

Objective reality goes back to the concept of commonly agreed upon reality. In this level, all of our little universes overlap to form a larger body of the whole. The knitting together of all of our You realities creates the physical world. Objective reality is the place where our thoughts mingle in the form of language. This interaction through language is the means by which we collectively begin to subtly alter our own reality and the reality of others around us.

Within the subtle layers of the objective reality we find part of the collective unconscious. Though this part is just a tendril of our collective, universal nature poking through, it is an important part of the whole. It can be easily argued that the collective unconscious is within the spiritual realm. The collective unconscious is the amalgam of all of the sentient minds that exist within this physical universe, which in turn forms the very medium by which matter and spirit can exist. It exists in a place where the language medium is both with and without words, a place where we all unconsciously agree upon the rules of the physical universe we interact in. The laws and rules established here are not static.

Since we have this overlap of perception and agreed upon rules, objective reality can also be divided into two classifications: hard- and soft-coded realities.

Hard-coded and Soft-coded Realities

Hard-coded realities are the physical and natural laws. These hard-coded realities are not alterable. You can take a table and cut it in two. This action does not alter the hard-coded reality. Turing the table into a car or melting it with your will would. To change hard-coded reality, you must change the laws of nature and science. This is not necessarily impossible; it's just not within the scope of this book.

The scope of the work described in this book involves the alteration of soft-coded realities. Soft-coded realities are the elements of You that you have control of in the objective reality. They include your home, job, level of success, health, friends, and personal associations. These elements can be altered by making changes at the you level of subjective reality.

Soft-coded reality can be summed up in three statements:

- Your words reflect your thoughts.
- Your thoughts are your energy.
- Your reality is made up of your thoughts, words, and energy.

Simply stated, how you think and speak is how your life is. How you live your life determines how your reality is. If you change any of these small things—your words, thoughts, and energy—all of the bigger things change with it.

Spiritual Reality

The energy of your thoughts and being is that part of you that exists within the spiritual reality. Within the spiritual level of reality we find the true universal language. This language is made up of concepts and ideas. These concepts and ideas transmit from being to being in an instant. Within the spiritual reality, the meaning of concepts and ideas cannot be lost to personal interpretation.

We are never separate from this spiritual level of reality. We are all spiritual beings by nature, and we bring that nature with us into our everyday world. But we give these universal concepts and ideas words and identities in ways that suit our own perceptions. The many means of communication we have come to know in the physical world cannot describe spiritual concepts perfectly.

Because of this dichotomy of our spiritual and physical existences, we must explain concepts and ideas in ways we can communicate to others. These ways of communicating must be logical and fit within the agreed upon rules of hard-coded objective reality.

For example, we all agree that a beam of light that has a wavelength of 650 nm is called red. That wavelength is the light's hard-coded property, and we agree upon it. We also agree to communicate that property via the word *red*. And though we all seem to agree that the color red does not indicate calm or peace, we do not agree whether it means lust, anger, joy, or pain. This subjective interpretation of red is our spiritual connection to each other and the color.

When a medium perceives the color red in an aura or spirit, she does not actually see red light with a wavelength of 650 nm.

Rather, a process within her brain has turned spiritual information into information that can be perceived and processed within the confines of human understanding—in this case, a color. This red that the medium sees is associated with an emotion. When she shares her perception of this red with others, then subjective reality begins. As the information is processed through others' imagination filters, each person interprets it differently. Some might imagine the "red" emotion to be anger, some might think it is lust, and others might think it is vivacity.

Spiritual information can be perceived not only as colors, but also as shapes, forms, or words. Although three people may receive the same spiritual information, each will perceive that information in a way that is real to him or her. One person will see red, another will feel a wave of heat, a third may hear the sound of fire. The difference is not in the spiritual information, but in the way each person's imagination filter works. Spiritual reality is also where the majority of the collective unconscious resides. In spiritual reality, all minds exist and overlap. Our perceptions and understandings mingle to create a collective whole. This is why communication in the spiritual realm is

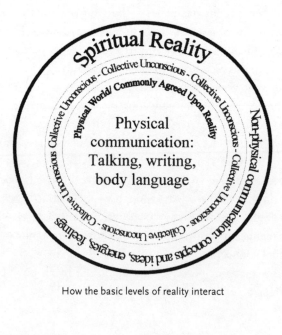

How the basic levels of reality interact

easy and complete. Within this pool of activity come the agreements about the nature of objective and spiritual realities.

Ginnic Reality

The final level of reality is Ginnic reality, the realm of existence that existed before there was anything else. Here, in this primal level of existence, there was nothing and everything all at once. This reality was the birthplace of ideas and concepts.

The ancient Norse people called this level of reality *Ginnungagap* and wrote epic poems and prose on the nature of gods within this place. Many ancient cultures have a very similar concept—a place of nothingness from whence all else was created. The Greeks called it Chaos; other beliefs called it darkness.

Ginn is an Old Norse word that means "ancient" and "universal." (It is used to form various other words, including *Ginnregin*, the term for the highest and most ancient of ruling gods [*regin* is "rulers"], and *Ginnhelog*, meaning "ancient holy" [*helog* is "holy"].) The Norse word *unga* means "young." *Gap* means just as it does in English. Therefore, *Ginnungagap* is the ancient/holy, younger gap.

It is within this gap that fire and ice mingled to create the building blocks of the universe. We do have a modern scientific understanding of these concepts. The fire, seen by the ancients, might be the fusion that takes place in stars. It may even be the Big Bang. The ice concept can be found in the notion of absolute zero. The various states of matter in the physical world exist between these extremes.

In the Prose Edda, Odin, in the guise of Harr, tells of the location of the hall of *Gimle*, a place of existence two levels above the realm of gods, mankind, and spirits:

> So it is said, that another heaven is to the south and up from this heaven and it is called Andlang (extensive). A third heaven that is one up from there and it is called Vidhblainn (wide blue). And in that heaven we believe this place is there. It is the Light elves, we believe, that now live in that place.

These realms of existence—Andlang and Vidhblainn—represent the Ginnic level of reality. These are places where the understanding that takes place in the spiritual realm would be remedial. Physical and spiritual realities offer no way of understanding the beings or processes in these places. This level of existence is mentioned to give you an understanding of the nature of realities we live within and where we all come from.

"You" and the Layers of Reality

The matter in the physical world is made up of particles of light that are bonded together. This concept is the basis of quantum physics. We have learned that the atom, the most basic form of matter, is mostly empty space. Within this space we find electrons, protons, and neutrons. The building blocks of these smaller particles are quarks, darks, neutrinos, and many other subatomic particles. These nanoparticles are nothing more than blips of lights behaving in specific ways.

A good way of looking at spiritual reality is as a realm of light and energy. The beings that exist within this realm are beings of radiant light. You are a being of radiant light existing within a body made up of light particles. The light of the spiritual realm is that of concepts, ideas, and connectedness.

The Ginnic level of existence is made up of a substance unknown to all science. That substance condenses into the ideas and concepts of the light of the spiritual universe. These light sources then condense into the particles that become matter.

All of the layers of existence have a connection to you. The Ginnic existence condenses into the light of spiritual existence. That light of the spiritual existence condenses into the matter of physical existence. You are the ultimate condensation of all that is considered holy in the universe. This means that you are inherently a pure, divine spiritual being, capable of anything you set your mind to.

Language Is the Key

Since, by nature, we are conscious beings, the reality we exist in must be interpreted through means understandable to the conscious mind. Through the ages, we have developed a concise means of interpreting the reality we perceive. Our senses perceive reality with a nonconscious means. We have sensory memory that lasts only a few seconds. The moment our eyes sense a beam of light, that information is stored, for only a brief moment, in the eyes. That information is also passed, that same instant, to the occipital cortex of the brain. There, that information is nothing but blips of electricity being transmitted through synapses. The brain takes the full amount of electrical information in as a random and meaningless bundle. Then your conscious mind interprets that bundle of information as something relevant to its past experience, but only if it is aware that it received the information. Meanwhile, the subconscious is always aware of it and stores the information in a way it can interpret.

The relevance to past experience is the most important part of the reception of information. All of reality that we come in contact with is interpreted and stored based on perception. Studies being done today show that all memories may be false. This means information received by the senses is interpreted in a way that makes sense to the conscious and unconscious mind regardless of what really happened. This selective process of interpretation and storage comes from the past experiences and training that the person has gone through.

To gain this past experience, we rely on the physical form of information gathering offered to us from birth: language. The language we speak, the way we form sentences, and the words we use in those sentences precode the brain to receive information in a certain way. Once that information is received and stored, we have a subjective interpretation of objective reality.

This interpretation is also how we start defining what makes up you. Two people can see the exact same events, and their interpretation of the results can differ dramatically. This difference has a continuing effect on each of their psyches—an effect that could easily make their individual views of the world strikingly different. This difference has each of them living inside a completely different subjective reality within the same objective universe.

This process of interpreting objective reality in a subjective way is analogous to carving marble. A large block of marble represents the realities we work with. The hard-coded, commonly agreed upon objective reality defines this block with certain unchangeable characteristics. It is white with dark streaks; it is cold, hard, and heavy; it also holds its shape until a hard striking force, such as a chisel, meets it. Our subjective interpretation is represented in the different ways various people see this stone. For some, this marble is impossible to work with. Others see it as an easy challenge to manipulate. One person is never able to decide what will effectively come out of it. If Michelangelo were to look at this marble, he would look for the form within and carve away the rest. The subjective reality and the you also come into play in what shapes different people see within this marble. One person could see a human figure, another might see an animal, and yet another may see a geometric shape. We all will see the shape within the marble differently, but the marble is still marble.

Using language is like carving the marble. The language one uses, the sentence structures, and the words are like various tools. For example, a person's word toolbox may be filled with phrases like "I cannot," "I will never be able to," "it is impossible," and "I do not deserve anything good." This is like carving a monument of impossibilities. The shape of the monument represents a life of loss, underachievement, and disappointment. Other people observing this monument of impossibility may agree with the statement it makes. Just as others observing the monument agree to the monument's purpose, so too can they agree with the statements a person makes about himself. This all reinforces the person's belief about what he cannot do.

When this person realizes the monument he has created, he is given the opportunity to trade in his toolbox for a new one. Now this person's word toolbox will include phrases such as, "I deserve good things," "I am a good person," "it may be difficult, but I love the challenge," and "I can do it." Using phrases like these carves a monument of possibilities. Those who observe this monument of success will agree that the success it is depicting is good. They may even be motivated by that image of success and let it become an inspiration to a better life.

The world we live in is as unchangeable as the physical properties of the marble, but just as you can change the shape of the marble, you can also change the way you see the world. While you cannot stop the fact you need to breathe air, eat food, drink water, or interact with people, you can change the way you do all of these things. You choose the quality of your air based on where you are. You decide what foods you eat, where you get your water from, and how you interact with people. All of these changes start with the conscious belief that you can change.

Change is not automatic, nor is it always easy. But the change is possible.

You begin changing your view of the world by changing the language you use on a daily basis. Start by changing negative phrasing to positive ones. As you change your words, your thoughts change. As you change your thoughts, your energy changes. This energy shift is the subtle effect needed to alter the reality around you. How you think, speak, and live will literally affect the world around you. It is not just your perception or other people's perception of you that will change, but also actual events. New and beneficial situations will be drawn to you. Where you once had bad luck, you will now have good luck. Where you once failed, you will now succeed. The things that went astray will now follow the pattern you need them to. All of these improvements are possible when you become aware of the words and sentences you use on a daily basis and change them in positive ways.

Cultures and Languages

The many cultures of the world see and interpret everything very differently based on the languages they use to communicate.

For example, both Sanskrit and Hebrew have sacred and spiritual uses. The letters of these languages have individual meanings as well as phonetic values. These meanings have spiritual energies associated with them. The very act of writing in Sanskrit or Hebrew is a sacred act of communication—communication not only with people but also with the energy of the letters. We can imagine that Sanskrit and Hebrew speakers may have more of a focus on spiritual matters.

It has been commented that Germanic languages are excellent for communicating complex concepts in a precise way that can be especially useful for science and mathematics. By their very nature these languages combine words together to form complex meanings. For example, the German word for time, *Zeit*, and the German word for ghost, *Geist* are combined into *Zeitgeist*—literally, the "spirit of the time." We could then apply that term to the overall feeling or mood for a particular moment. It could be said that Germanic speakers tend to think and speak in detailed and technical ways. They purposefully speak with specific intentions.

Hebrew, Sanskrit, and Germanic languages all can convey the same exact information, but they do so very differently and offer different focuses. The people from the cultures that use these languages may interpret and communicate the same events very differently. Thus, people living in these cultures have very different views of reality. Their subjective interpretation of the objective reality will have a different impact on the you and You levels of their being.

But even within these languages, mood and inflection can be altered, at the personal level, to modify a person's own subjective reality. Changing negative phrasing to positive phrasing will completely change the world around you, no matter what language you speak.

Making the Change

Changing one's own reality is possible and easy to do. Changing the words one uses from negatives to positives will alter how the world interacts with that person. Further and more complicated changes are also possible.

Although one can charge forth at full speed, making these changes willy-nilly with no plan in mind, this unstructured process will not necessarily produce long-lasting or predictable results. But within the ancient Nordic spiritual system of the runes are structured, tried-and-true ways of making these changes. The runes form the written language used by the ancient Germanic peoples. The runes were found throughout all of Scandinavia, Germany, England, Ireland, Scotland, and any place where the ancient Scandinavians traveled. When the Vikings set sail, they took the runes with them. When the ancient Swedes went overland into Russia and the Middle East, they took the runes with them. Runes carved by these peoples can be found throughout most of the known ancient world.

We will explore runes in three different ways. The first will be an exploration of their use in objective reality. You will learn who used them, how these people used them, and what they meant. Then you will take the runes and explore them using concepts of you and You. The meanings for the runes were relevant and valuable to the ancient Scandinavian people. These same concepts work for today's people, but especially for those who speak a language that is descended from the Proto-Germanic language, such as English, German, Swedish, Norwegian, and Danish. This is so because the very nature of the language used for ancient rune workings (i.e., the phonetic values of the runes and the words used on rune stones) is alive today in these languages. We see this with words like fee, mother, father, and stone.

Finally, you will be given the opportunity to understand the runes from your own unique perspective and see how they apply internally and externally. You will also discover successful techniques to use these runes to change your reality.

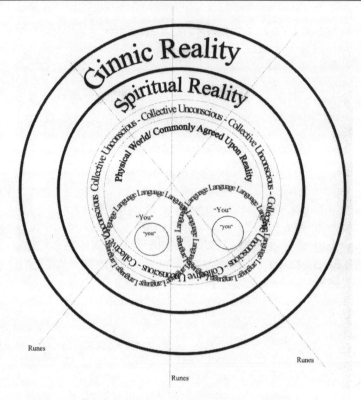

Exercise 1: Removing the Words

The essence of runes exists in a place without words. We understand this existence as the place of sensory information, spirituality, and the collective unconscious.

This exercise will teach you to remove the words from your internal communication. Being able to communicate internally without words is a skill that will be used throughout the remainder of this book. Those that have acquired this skill have noticed some interesting effects: they find it easier to receive spiritual communication and external inspiration. This is because the language of those in the spiritual realms does not use words.

To begin, gather three objects: one object you are intimately familiar with and two everyday objects that you barely notice. The first could be a photograph, memento, your watch, or anything that you connect with at a conscious level. The other two objects could be pencils or pens, keys, or anything you pay little attention to on a daily basis.

There is no need to write down anything or log your progress with this exercise. Because you will be exploring an internal language without words, you will have nothing to record. All you need to do is notice what is happening internally.

Take your first object and notice it in every possible way. Notice what it looks like, feels like, and what memories might be tied to it. Think about how others use it and how you use it. Now repeat this process but avoid using any words with your mental description. Notice the object's color, texture, and weight. Do not think about these things in words.

Soon you will notice that you have an intrinsic understanding of this object without any words. Repeat this process until you are comfortable understanding and experiencing this object in its entirety without words. What you have done is create a simple wordless packet of information that can be expanded into the many words that you would use to communicate.

Once you feel comfortable with the internal, wordless description of your familiar object, repeat the exercise with the other two.

When you are beginning to feel comfortable with the ideology of these objects, begin to imagine what it would take to transmit this sort of information. Think of this packet of wordless information as a compressed computer file. Once we upload that file to another computer, that computer decompresses the file to read the file in its entirety. This is how spiritual communication and inspiration are received from external sources. This same method is how one receives communication from the spiritual reality. A spirit simply places a packet of wordless information into the mind of a person. This information is then uncompressed and processed through the person's imagination filter using terms, images, or any other relevant sensory information that the person is accustomed to using in his or her own subjective reality.

THE NATURE OF RUNES

At one time runes were used to communicate all manner of information. Since they existed in a time period when there were few literate people, the use of runes gained a mystical function. In their most basic form, runes were the only physical means of conveying spoken language. There are many archeological examples of runic writing, ranging from shipping tags to large stones. Carved runes were also used in talismans for magical purposes.

For the purposes of the work ahead, we will acknowledge the communication aspect of the runes. However, we also will be looking to the ancient wisdom for the magical uses of the runes.

The magic of the Nordic peoples took on two forms: *Galdr* and *Seidh*. Seidh is considered a shamanic practice, and its earliest practitioners were primarily female. (There are only a few recorded examples of men performing Seidh.) The action, or rather inaction, of Seidh is to enter an altered state of consciousness through trance. Seidh's primary use is for prophecy. Seidh was also used to create sendings. A sending is a form of spiritual entity that is sent to another's home to cause mischief and unrest. Finally, Seidh is also used for possessory rites. Today, we might call this practice trance mediumship, in which the practitioner goes into a deep trance and allows a spirit or deity to speak through her or his body. The techniques of Seidh require training and practice to be done safely and effectively.

Galdr is rune magic and was primarily used by men. The term *Galdr* means "to utter" or "to sing." The names of the runes, or just their phonetic values, were sung when Galdr was performed. There is good reason to believe that the ancient practice of rune magic involved both carving and singing the runes. We know the runes were carved, as we have ample archeological evidence of this. Rune scripts, which had magical uses, were carved onto stones, weapons, jewelry, and even people.

An Icelandic book called the *Galdrabok*, or "Book of Galdrs," used nonrunic and runic symbols embedded with specific intentions and energies. It was simply a book of magic spells used in Old Iceland.

Just as there were Seidh workers, there were skilled men trained in the art of runes. They were called upon to carve runes for all manner of use. We see great stone monuments throughout Scandinavia. Many of these stones bear the phrase *Ek Erilaz. Ek* means "I"; *Erilaz* is "a rune master." This phrase suggests that there may have been a guild that trained people in the proper use of runes for secular and sacred practices.

One such sacred use was that of divination. When Tacitus wrote of his journeys and interactions with the Germanic peoples, he described Germanic people performing divination. Whether he did or did not observe runes being used in the divination ritual is debatable, but many people today use the procedure he described to do runic divination. First, a branch would be cut off a nut- or fruit-bearing tree and sliced into strips. Onto each strip a sacred sign would be carved. Then these strips were thrown onto a white cloth. The priest or father of the family would look to the sky and pull three strips. One at a time, he would tell the meanings of the signs on the strips he had pulled.

Runic Anatomy

To understand runes, we must understand their makeup. The runes we see carved and written are not actually the runes themselves, but staves. Staves represent the runes' energies and the phonetic values. The phonetic value is a vibrational energy used to tap into the runic energy. The name of the rune is simply a mnemonic reminder of the purpose and function of the runic energy. Runic anatomy has three components: shape, name, and meaning.

Shape

All runes have a physical shape. The shape a rune has is analogous to the human body. Just like human energy, the runic energy needs to exist in a physical form in order to reside in the physical universe.

Runes have both an ideographic nature and a pictographic nature. The ideogram serves simply as a reminder of the idea of the rune's nature, phonetic value, and energy where the pictograph may represent an image of the meaning of the rune. For example, Perhro, ᛉ, has only an ideographic nature, where Berkana, ᛒ, has an ideographic and pictographic nature.

Berkana, ᛒ, represents the birch tree and female fertility. Some suggest the shape of this rune is that of a pregnant woman's breast and belly. The rune Thurisaz, ᚦ, meaning "thorn," is shaped like a thorn on a branch. Sometimes it takes a little imagination to see the pictographic natures of the runes. Some are readily apparent.

The shape of the runes also has a pragmatic nature. They needed to be carved into wood and stone with tools that were not the easiest to carve with. Most of the runes have a strong vertical line, which aided in their carving. The ancient rune masters would carve two horizontal channels into the stone. When they carved the rune, they would carve just a straight vertical line, or stave, from one channel to the other. Then they would carve the smaller lines angling off the main stave.

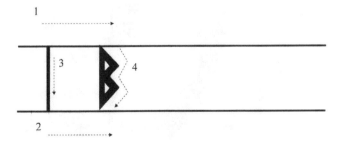

1. Top channel; 2. Bottom channel; 3. Vertical stave; 4. Angled cuts to shape the rune

This carving technique is evident with the evolution of runes. The first runic alphabet, or Elder Futhark, had twenty-four runes. As the language evolved and more people became literate, the new alphabet, or Younger Futhark, had only sixteen runes, and all but one, sol (ᛂ), had one solid straight line as its stave. The only explanation for the increase of words but the decrease in letters is that there were more literate people looking for an easier way to carve runes. Think of this change as analogous to printing versus writing in cursive. We can write faster and easier in cursive than in print, just as it became easier to carve the sixteen new runes than the original twenty-four.

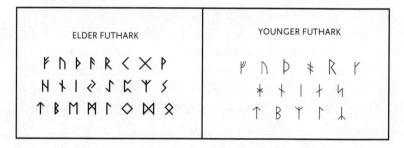

ELDER FUTHARK	YOUNGER FUTHARK
ᚠ ᚢ ᚦ ᚨ ᚱ ᚲ ᚷ ᚹ ᚺ ᚾ ᛁ ᛃ ᛇ ᛈ ᛉ ᛋ ᛏ ᛒ ᛖ ᛗ ᛚ ᛜ ᛞ ᛟ	ᚠ ᚢ ᚦ ᚬ ᚱ ᚴ ᚼ ᚾ ᛁ ᛅ ᛋ ᛏ ᛒ ᛘ ᛚ ᛦ

Name

Every rune also has a name that represents its specific energy. The names that the runes took on were relevant to the people who spoke Old Norse. When exploring the names of the runes, a good deal of cultural relativity is needed for us to understand them.

Let's take Fehu as an example. Its name literally means "cattle." To the Old Norse people, cattle were a sign of wealth and a means for trade. Later on, the energy of Fehu had more to do with money and wealth. Today we may have difficulty getting the connection between cattle and wealth.

The names and functions of the runes we use today mainly come from the rune poems. There are four poems in total: the Anglo-Saxon, the Old Norwegian, the Icelandic, and the *Abecedarium Nordmanicum*. The Anglo-Saxon poem describes the twenty-four runes of the Elder Futhark, with an additional five runes unique to the language of the Anglo-Saxons. The Old Norwegian and the Icelandic describe the sixteen-rune Younger Futhark. Each of their sixteen stanzas starts with the name of the rune. For example:

<u>Feoh</u> byþ frofur fira gehwylcum
<u>Wealth</u> is a comfort to all men

The Abecedarium Nordmanicum also describes the sixteen-rune Futhark, but not with sixteen different stanzas. Instead, it is a short, one-stanza poem, and each of the names of the runes is just a word.

For the most part, the name of the rune was used as a mnemonic to its phonetic value, or sound.

RUNE	PHONETIC VALUE/SOUND	NAME
ᚠ	*f*	Fehu
ᚢ	*u* (*oo*)	Uruz
ᚦ	*th*	Thurisaz

All but one of the runes' names start with the rune's phonetic value. The exception is Elhaz (ᛉ). It represents the *z* sound that comes only at the end of certain words.

It is the belief of many rune workers that the phonetic value of the rune is the part that is sung. If you were to invoke the energies of Fehu, you would utter the *f* sound continuously. Other workers sing the entire name of the rune. It is best to go with the method you feel most attracted to.

Meaning

Often, but not always, the name of the rune was directly tied in with its meaning. It is important to differentiate the meaning from the name of the rune. Often the runes' names had little direct relevance to the meaning and nature of the rune. Some of the runic names are the same as the names of trees: *Berkana* (ᛒ), "birch"; *Ansuz* (ᚠ), "oak"; *Eihwaz* (ᛇ), "yew." These trees served as metaphors for the actual ideas and energies of these runes.

The only way to understand the connection of names and energies would be to try to understand the way the ancient Nordic people experienced and understood their world. There are graduate programs that are designed to help people do that. However, we will not need to go that far to discern the meanings of the runes for our purposes.

Ultimately, the meanings of the runes are tied into that part of the runes that cannot be expressed with words. The meanings are offered to the students of runes as a means of delving deeper in to the mysteries of the world around them.

It is the combination of the three parts of the runes—shape, name, and meaning—that gave ancient rune workers access to the deeper natures of their world. The names of the runes served as a mnemonic to the meaning and sound of the rune. The sounds uttered altered the workers' consciousness so they could tune their energy to the nature of the rune. By removing the words from the meaning of the rune, the ancient rune masters were able to go deeper into the causal nature of the world. From there they could make their changes.

Origin of the Runes

There are two roads to understanding the origin of the runes: the historical road and mythological road. The truths lying behind both have been lost in obscurity through the passage of time.

At the time of the origin of runes in Scandinavia (250 BC), there was almost no recorded history. What we have today are pieces and parts from archeology and literature. None of these sources exactly match or have any definitive answers, and the lack of concise information leads to the deeper mystery of the runes.

Historical Origin

Many scholars tie the term *Erilaz*, the word found on many rune stones and denoting that a rune master carved that stone, to the origin of Scandinavian writing. And the origin of the word *Erilaz* can give us a clue as to the origin of the runes.

There are scholars who link the word *Erilaz* with the name of the Heruli. The origin of the Heruli is shrouded in mystery, and fraught with debate. In the year AD 551 the historian Jordanes wrote that the Heruli were expelled from their homelands. These homelands were thought to be what are now Denmark and Gotland (an island off the coast of Sweden). Jordanes does not specify a time period when the Heruli were expelled.

From there, the Erilaz/Heruli became mercenaries who traveled all over mainland Europe. There are reports of their travel from Germany, along the Rhine, to the Aegean Sea. They battled with the Huns and served with the Byzantine guard. There is an account saying that they were one of the mercenary tribes who served Rome and eventually fought alongside the other Gothic tribes that defeated Rome.

All of the Heruli's recorded travels range from the third through the fifth centuries. There is also evidence that suggests the Heruli did indeed return to their homelands after the time of their expulsion. Perhaps it is through this time period that the Heruli learned of writing and taught the people of their homelands to carve words into stone. This system of writing evolved into what we now know as runes.

The greatest debate about the supposed origin of the runes as it relates to the Heruli and their exploits is over the time period of their travels. It does not exactly match the documentation of runic objects. Some theorists suggest that runic carving started in 250 BCE. Archeologically, however, there was a surge of rune carvings on the Danish isle of Zealand in the third century. This upswing in carvings ties in nicely with the timeline and location of the Heruli's travels.

Mythological Origin

The mythological origin of the runes is perhaps more poignant than their historical origins. While the historical origin of the runes is supported by many sources, there are only two mythological sources for their origin: the Poetic Edda and the Prose Edda. These are a collection of mythological tales recorded in Iceland during the Middle Ages. The Poetic Edda is a collection of thirty-five poems recorded in about AD 1100 by Saemund Sigfusson. About a century later, a man named Snorri Sturlusson composed these poems into two narratives (and a small collection of poems) dubbed the Prose Edda. Contained within the Eddas are the mythological origins of the universe, the nature of gods, mankind, dwarves, elves, giants, and eventually the destruction of all things known.

Both Eddas agree upon the same account of the runes' origin; however, the interpretation of the events of the mythology are in question. There is one Eddic poem that tells of the discovery of the runes, and that is the Havamal, or "The Sayings of the High One" (Odin). Another poem, the Rigsthula, "The Song of Rig," tells how runic wisdom was brought to mankind.

The Havamal is the longest of all the poems in the Poetic Edda. The first two-thirds of the poem tell of the morality of Old Norse society. The last part is called the *Runatals Thattr Odhni*, or "Odin's Song of the Runes." It tells of his discovery of the runes:

> *I know I hung, on the windy tree*
> *All of nine nights*
> *Wounded by spear, and given to Odin*
> *Myself a sacrifice to myself*
> *Bound to the tree, no man knows*
> *Where the roots run*
>
> *Without bread, nor with horn*
> *I looked down*
> *Took up the runes, took them wailing*
> *and fell back after*

What we have is the self-sacrifice of Odin as he hung upon the world tree, Yggdrasil, for nine nights. Odin is the chieftain among all the gods who is known for his wisdom, shamanic abilities, poetry, and leadership in battle. The world tree, Yggdrasil, is the Axis Mundi or cosmic pole that holds all of the universes together. The action of hanging on a tree is thought to have been an ancient shamanic practice. The action of a god hanging from the great universal tree is thought to bring a deep understanding of ancient wisdom from the Ginnic reality. During his trial on the tree, Odin sees the runes in the depths of the universe, reaches out, grabs them, then falls from the tree.

Further on in the poem:

> *Runes must you find, and staves of counsel*
> *Very large staves*
> *Very strong staves*
> *Colored by the Fimblthular*
> *Made by the Ginnregin*
> *and carved by Hropt*

> *Odin for the gods, for Elves Dain*
> *Dvalinn for dwarves*
> *Asvith for Etins*
> *and I carved some myself*

What is described here is the true origin of the runes. The *Ginnregin,* the ancient holy rulers who existed before the gods, shaped or made the runes. Once the runes were made, the *Fimblthular,* "the Great Singer," colored, or stained, them by giving them lifeblood. (*Fimbul* means "great," and *thule* literally means "singer." The thule was a priest or rune worker.) *Hropt* is one of the many names of Odin. When the poem notes that Hropt carved the staves, it means Odin gave the runes physical form.

The mythological process of shaping and giving the runes life tells us a few things. All of this happened in the Ginnic reality, during the time before time. Odin is one of the three gods responsible for forming the physical universe and its human inhabitants.

It is reasonable to assume that his discovery of the runes took place after this creation process. This fact tells us that the nature of the runic energy permeates through all the various levels of reality, from the Ginnic to the you level.

The first stanza also tells us that because of the staining process, the runic energy is a living force. They are not unlike human souls, except that each of the runic energies is a singular, solitary focus.

The second stanza indicates that runes have been disseminated throughout the universe, and there are many different species of beings that have different sets of runes. There is no indication which set humans have, but there is another poem, The Rigsthula, that tells of runes being taught to a man by a god.

The Rigsthula tells how the god Heimdall comes to Earth disguised as a traveler named Rig. Rig visits three different homes. They range from a home with a dirt floor, closed door, and meager food to an elaborate home with a wide-open door and great food. In each of these three homes he stays three nights.

Over those three nights, Rig teaches the mother and father of each family with counsel they could understand. These visits resulted in the three classes found in Old Norse society. To the lowest class, Rig sired the line of Thralls, or the servant class. With the farmers, or middle class, Rig sired the line of Karls, or free men. To the family with the best of things, Rig sired the class of Earls, or royalty.

Rig's son with the royal class was called Earl. As Earl grew, he married and had a son he named Kon. As Kon grew and became wise in the world, Rig returned and taught runes to Kon. The Poetic Edda describes this meeting of Kon and Rig, and below is the description of the manner of runes Rig taught:

> But young Kon knew runes
> Living runes and olden runes
> More he knew, to help pregnant women
> To blunt edges, and calm the seas
>
> He learned bird speak, to calm the fires
> Calming the seas and soothing sorrows
> He had the strength and energy of eight men

He, with the Earl Rig, contended runes
Battled in wits and better knew the runes
Then he won, and got to possess
The name Rig and rune knowledge

What is interesting here are the descriptions of uses of the runes: to help pregnant women, calm the sea, quench fires, and soothe sorrows. These charms are also told of in a further part of the Havamal and again in the poem the Sigrdrifumal.

We can glean from these descriptions that the runes were used as active tools of transformation. They aided members of society. Also noted in the Rigsthula is the fact runes were taught to the ruling class. Certainly in today's society, no knowledge is reserved for people of any specific class or financial level, but a thousand years ago, the freeman and servant classes did a majority of the work. They were educated, but only to a point. They needed to do the work assigned to them or what was necessary for survival. Only the ruling class had the time to invest in the study of the deeper levels of mysteries, to apply themselves to meditation and study of the runes.

Today, in the Western world, a vast majority of us live in conditions that would have exceeded the standards of the royal class a thousand years ago. Because of the education we now enjoy, the understanding from the deeper levels of the runes is accessible to us.

One more point made by the Rigsthula:

Then spoke that crow, sitting alone on a bough
"Why should you, young Kon, tame the birds?
Rather, you should ride horses
[Ride horses], and fell warriors"

"With Dan and Danp, a clear hall
Greater estates than you have
They know well how to ride the keel
Edges the prove and inflict wounds"

As noted above, Kon could understand the language of the birds. Here a crow tells him to conquer the lands of Dan and Danp—that is, the land of the Danes. The Heruli returned to their homeland of Denmark and Gotland with the secrets of the runes. There is a remarkable correlation here to the historical and mythological origin of the runes.

Runic Values

Runes permeate all layers of reality, from the Ginnic to the most finite. In fact, the word *rune* means "mystery." The secrets of writing and the Norse spiritual system were taught only to a select few. Today, because of the advances of technology and education, these secrets are available to all. We can learn from what the ancients knew. After all, it was through their efforts and sacrifices that we even exist today. What kept them going, through thick and thin, was their value system. We have seen that cultures can pass on an understanding of reality through the language they speak. As our English language is an evolution of Old Norse, many ancient Nordic values are still alive within us today. This value system can be learned from the runes.

The ancients' value system was their connection to the world around them. It connected them to each other, the land, and the spiritual realms. Many of these connections we still make today. Some of their values included wealth, health, fierceness, and knowledge. These values correlate with the meanings of the first four runes: Fehu (ᚠ), "wealth"; Uruz (ᚢ), "health"; Thurisaz (ᚦ), "fierceness"; Ansuz (ᚨ), "knowledge." We hold true to these same values today. We all value our income and the status of our health. Boldness and fierceness are successful traits in sports and business. Many believe we have moved from the industrial age into the information age. This makes the value of Ansuz (ᚨ) paramount to our time in society.

Many of the names of the runes have evolved into modern English words. For example: *Fehu* became, *Fe'*, which became the English word *fee*. All of these terms have a connotation of the exchange of money. *Ansuz*, the root of which is *Anza*, evolved into *Ansur*, which evolved into the modern *answer*.

In addition to the names of the runes, many of the words carved into the ancient rune stones are still used regularly today. Words such as mother, father, sister, brother were spelled *mothr*, *fathr*, *sistr*, and *brothr*. The pronunciation of these words is virtually unchanged since they were first carved on the rune stones, over 1,000 years ago.

In Jelling, Denmark, are two great stones carved with runes. The larger of the two stones was carved by Harald Bluetooth in memory of his mother and father. On this stone, we find the carved words *mothr* (mother) and *fathr* (father). In addition is the word *Konunger*, the Danish word for king. It is also the name given to the young son of Earl who was skilled in the use of runes.

Another example of English words derived from Old Norse is the modern names for the days of the week. Sunday is the day of the sun. It is named after the Norse goddess Sunna. Monday is the moon's day, and the moon is named for the Norse god Mani. Tuesday is Tiu's day. Tiu, or Tyr, is the one-handed Norse god who bound the forces of destructive chaos. Wednesday is Woden's day; Woden is another name for Odin. Thursday is Thor's day, the day of the thunder god. Friday is Freyr's day, named for the Norse god of prosperity and fertility. Of these days, five have direct runic correlations. Also note that the sounds of the runes are alliterative of the names of the gods they represent:

Sunday	Sowilo (S)	*s*	the sun
Tuesday	Tiwaz ($\uparrow$)	*t*	Tyr
Wednesday	Ansuz (F)	*a/o*	Odin
Thursday	Thurisaz (P)	*th*	Thor
Friday	Inguz ($\diamondsuit$)	*ng*	Freyr

From all of these examples we can easily see that the value system bestowed to the runes is still alive within the language we use today. And because the values are exactly the same and always will be, we have direct access to the same spiritual forces used by the ancient Norse. We may call the values by different names, we may address them differently, but the forces are universal and accessible to anyone, in any time period.

These same concepts are accessible through different languages. Tibetan, Sanskrit, and Hebrew use the same concepts to tap into these same energies. While every symbol of these languages has a phonetic value, it also contains a conscious mnemonic for a specific spiritual energy. All of these language systems are valuable and correct in their execution. What makes them different is their accessibility to the cultures that speak them. English speakers may or may not find it difficult to connect with Hebrew or Sanskrit. Runes tap into the same energies as these other systems, but they may be more accessible to those who speak languages that descended from Old Norse.

The Elder Futhark

The Elder Futhark, used from 250 BCE until about 500 CE, is so called because the first six runes form the word Futhark:

ᚠ	ᚢ	ᚦ	ᚨ	ᚱ	ᚲ
F	U	TH	A	R	K

These same six runes appear in the same order with slight variations in the Younger Futhark and the Elder Futhark. The Younger Futhark was used in Scandinavia from about 500 CE until 1639 CE, when it was banned by the church. During this time period, many of the runes changed shape and varied slightly in phonetic value. There was never a standardized runic spelling for words carved with runes. The Elder Futhark was in use throughout Scandinavia from 250 BCE until 500 CE The Elder Futhark runes are used within the context of this book. Here are the runes of the Elder Futhark in the traditional arrangement of three *aetts* (families).

Rune	ᚠ	ᚢ	ᚦ	ᚨ	ᚱ	ᚲ	ᚷ	ᚹ
Phonetic Value	F	U	Th	A	R	K	G	W
Rune	ᚺ	ᚾ	ᛁ	ᛃ	ᛇ	ᛈ	ᛉ	ᛋ
Phonetic Value	H	N	I	J/Y	Ei	P	Z	S
Rune	ᛏ	ᛒ	ᛖ	ᛗ	ᛚ	ᛝ	ᛞ	ᛟ
Phonetic Value	T	B	E	M	L	Ng	D	O

You may note that many of these runes bear a striking resemblance to letters of the modern English alphabet. That is no coincidence. Just as English is an amalgam of Latin and Germanic words, so too is our alphabet an amalgam of Roman letters and Norse runes. You will notice Fehu, ᚠ, looks like *F*; Raido, ᚱ, looks like *R*; Hagalaz, ᚺ, looks like *H*; Sowilo, ᛋ, looks like *S*; and so on. The phonetic values of these runes have remained constant for over two thousand years. This constant nature of the phonetic values gives us an easy connection to the spirit of long ago. As we sing the sounds of the runes, we cause a temporal resonation with the ancient rune singers. Their Galdr and the Galdr of today create a wave, increasing the potency of rune songs sung throughout time. As of this moment, you are connecting with the ancient ways of the runes. As you say their names and sing their sounds, you join in a long line of Galdr singers creating a grand, universal chorus.

The Twenty-four Runes

FEHU

Alternate names: Feoh, Fe', Feu

Phonetic value: *f*

Translations: Wealth, cattle, fee

Icelandic rune poem:

> *Wealth source of discord*
> *among kinsmen*
> *and fire of the sea*
> *and path of the serpent*

Anglo-Saxon rune poem:

> *Wealth is a comfort to all men;*
> *yet must every man bestow it freely,*
> *if he wish to gain honor in the sight of the Lord.*

Norwegian rune poem:

> *Wealth is a source of discord among kinsmen;*
> *the wolf lives in the forest.*

The idea behind this rune is wealth and transferable assets. The word *Fehu* literally means "cattle." To the ancient Nordic people, cattle were essential to life. Their diet consisted primarily of meats and dairy, the source of which were cattle. Because the old Scandinavian world was agrarian, the ruling class was composed of farmers, and the wealthiest farmers had the most cattle. Even the Viking warriors' main goal was to gain enough wealth to have a farm.

Cattle were also used as a primary source of trade before gold and silver became standard. As society progressed, the trade changed. With that change, the name and meaning of the rune Fehu also changed. In the Norse poetry an honorific title used for generous leaders was "ring breaker." It referred to the arm rings that a king or other such noble would wear. A common form of payment was for the king to break an arm ring and give it to his employees.

This concept of wealth was the source of discord that is spoken of in the Icelandic and Norwegian poems. The more wealth one had, the more he tended to flaunt it. This attitude led to jealousy. We still see this dynamic occurring today. As language evolved further, the name *Fehu* gave way to *Fe'*, the literal translation of which is "fee."

In modern concepts, think of the energy of Fehu as a medium of exchange. In its simplest form, Fehu's energy is that of money, including stocks and bonds, loans, or anything else to do with money. This energy also takes on the form of capital and payments, which need not always be money. For a person trying to lose weight, this payment is the exercise. For someone in school, this investment is time spent on studying.

The energy of Fehu is the transfer of anything of value. That payment can be given to a person, business, or even to one's self.

Alternate names: Ur, Uroz

Phonetic value: *u*

Translations: *Aurochs, dross, drizzle, shower*

Icelandic rune poem:

> *Lamentation of the clouds*
> *and ruin of the hay-harvest*
> *and abomination of the shepherd.*

Anglo-Saxon rune poem:

> *The aurochs is proud and has great horns;*
> *it is a very savage beast and fights with its horns;*
> *a great ranger of the moors, it is a creature of mettle.*

Norwegian rune poem:

> *Dross comes from bad iron;*
> *the reindeer often races over the frozen snow.*

To the ancients who used the Elder Futhark, the second rune represented the aurochs, ancient long-horned bison, the last of which was killed off in 1627 in Poland. The nature of this beast was primal and untamable. It is suggested by historical and literary sources that initiatory rites of young men involved killing an aurochs in one-on-one combat within a pit. One of the most remarkable features of the aurochs was its horns, which easily reached six feet in length. Certainly battle with such a beast would require great strength and cunning.

Associated with such a beast is the strength and vitality it contains. There are great legends of a warrior killing and eating the heart of a dragon; that warrior was bestowed with great strength, wisdom, and magical powers. The same could be thought of the aurochs. If one were to kill such a beast and eat it, then that beast's strength would manifest within him. The most common drinking vessel of the Viking era was the horn of a bull. The horns of the aurochs were most prized for their size. A man was thought to be great if he could drain an aurochs's horn full of mead in one go.

Looking through the poems, there seem to be conflicting meanings for this rune. The Icelandic poem tells of a rain that destroys harvests; the Norwegian poem tells of dross, or slag—unusable iron that comes from bad ore. The Anglo-Saxon poem describes the aurochs' physical and mental attributes. There seems to be little direct crossover here. Three different cultures interpret the same energy differently. An analogy may tie these three poems together: that of a bull in a china shop. The beast is large, powerful, and unruly. Surely any movement it makes would destroy the delicate finery of the shop, making it unusable and an abomination to the shop owner.

Today, this rune is effective for healing work. Think of taking all of the massive strength and vitality of the modern long-horn steer or American bison and pushing it into the body of a human. Think of this energy also as that of the primal, unfocused, and untamable beasts of the wild. Imagine what that energy would do to a human.

THURISAZ

Alternate names: Thorn, Thuris, Thurs

Phonetic value: *th*

Translations: *Giant/demon, thorn*

Icelandic rune poem:

> *Torture of women*
> *and cliff-dweller*
> *and husband of a giantess*

Anglo-Saxon rune poem:

> *The thorn is exceedingly sharp,*
> *an evil thing for any knight to touch,*
> *uncommonly severe on all who sit among them.*

Norwegian rune poem:

> *Giant causes anguish to women;*
> *misfortune makes few men cheerful.*

The essence of the third rune is in the alliterative nature of its seed sound, *th*. The relevant words would be *Thurs, Thor,* and *thunder.* To the ancient Norse, there were two major types of giants. The first were the massive creatures of nature called the Jotuns (see ᚺ, Hagalaz); these beings were analogous to mountains, valleys, and storms. The other type of giant was the Thurs. Examples of names of the Thurses include *Hati* ("hater") or *Angerboda* ("boding of anger"). These giants represent violent forms of energy that are destructive to humans, gods, and elves alike.

The gods, elves, and humankind all have a common protector. He is known as the Folk-warder, Thunderer, Red-beard, or, more commonly, Thor. Thor is a god not of war and battle but of protection. His main purpose is to protect the sanctity and peace of the realms of the gods and mankind. He is the son of Odin and Mother Earth. His main weapon is his mighty hammer, Mjollnir. The energy of Thor is brash and harsh; he acts first, thinks later. His actions and energy are homogenous with that of the Thurs. What holds him back from being purely destructive is the temperance he receives from his fellow gods. He gets his wisdom from Odin and sense of righteousness from Tyr (the binder of chaos).

There is a river that borders the lands of the gods and Thurses called Ifing. Elsa-Brita Titchenell, in her book *The Masks of Odin*, suggests that the name of this river is "doubt." This name can be taken, metaphorically, to mean that the only thing separating gods and Thurses is doubt. While the other gods enter their world using the rainbow bridge, Thor must traverse the river Ifing. Some Thurses eventually become recognized as gods. Skadi is one of the most famous. Even the high one, Odin, was once called a troll before his advancement into godhood. Perhaps these former giants successfully navigated their waters of doubt.

The shape of the rune suggests that of a thorn on a branch. Hence, one of its names is Thorn. We can think of the energy of Thurisaz not as that of a stationary thornbush foreboding any passage. Its energy is that of someone angrily holding a branch of thorns and thrashing it about wildly.

ANSUZ

Alternate names: Oss, Ansur

Phonetic value: *a/o*

Translations: *God, mouth, estuary, answer*

Icelandic rune poem:

> *Aged Gautr*
> *and prince of Ásgardr*
> *and lord of Vallhalla.*

Anglo-Saxon rune poem:

> *The mouth is the source of all language,*
> *a pillar of wisdom and a comfort to wise men,*
> *a blessing and a joy to every knight.*

Norwegian rune poem:

> *Estuary is the way of most journeys;*
> *but a scabbard is of swords.*

The essential energy of Ansuz comes from the Old Norse word *Anza*; it means "to answer." Thus, the energy of Ansuz is tied with spoken forms of communication. Foremost of all the Nordic gods for communication is Odin. One of his accomplishments was gaining the great mead Odhroerir, made of the blood of a murdered god named Kvas. It was said that Kvas could answer any question that was posed to him. He was the living repository of all knowledge. Kvas's blood was mixed with honey and water to make mead, and whosoever should drink of it could easily compose elegant poetry. Odin decided he needed that mead for himself. Once he obtained it, by tricking the giants, he took the form of an eagle and flew back to Asgardh (realm of the gods), holding the mead within his mouth. As he flew, some drops of this mead fell to Earth. The Poetic Edda says those drops of mead are called the poetasters' share. Thus poetry was sometimes called mead or wine.

From the Icelandic poem, we see this rune as named As. *As* is the Old Norse word for "god." (*Asynjur* is "goddess.") The description, "aged Gautr, prince of Asgardh and lord of Vallhalla," leaves no room for doubt that this poem is about Odin himself. It is curious that the writer chose to call Odin *Gautr*, the Old Norse term for the Goths. As you may remember, the Erilaz also were a tribe of the Goths. No doubt this poem is referring here to the connection between Odin and the Erilaz.

The Anglo-Saxon poem calls this rune Os, which translates to "mouth." There is an etymological connection between *As*, "god," and *Os*, "mouth." Again we have a connection with communication and a tie back to *anza* ("answer").

To sum up the energy of Ansuz, we must look at the aspects of Odin and of communication. They are closely tied. It is said that Odin eats of no food, only drinks wine. This is an allusion to wine/mead as poetry. The Old Norse held many secrets in their poetry in the form of kennings. Kennings were lyrical metaphors, such as calling a warrior an oak of battle. The use of kennings in poetry is similar to the mystery of the runes. When one understood the mythology, one understood the kennings. When one understands the nature of the runes, then one begins to understand the deeper mysteries of the universe.

The energy of Ansuz is that of the mysteries, and the understanding of these mysteries. This energy is manifest in the forms of communication, education, and the underlying power of the words.

RAIDO

Alternate names: Rad, Rauth

Phonetic value: *r*

Translations: *Wheel, journey, riding*

Icelandic rune poem:

> *Joy of the horsemen*
> *and speedy journey*
> *and toil of the steed.*

Anglo-Saxon rune poem:

> *Riding seems easy to every warrior while he is indoors*
> *and very courageous to him who traverses*
> > *the high-roads*
> *on the back of a stout horse.*

Norwegian rune poem:

> *Riding is said to be the worst thing for horses;*
> *Reginn forged the finest sword.*

Literally, *Raido* means "wheel." Manifest in the energies of Raido is the energy of travel. We see this connection in the translation of all three poems, which call Raido "riding." These words in the old tongues refer not only to the action of riding, but also to the vehicle in or on which one rides.

There are great literary, archeological, and artistic representations of what riding meant to the ancients. Thor traveled all over the lands in a chariot pulled by two goats. Freya, Freyr's sister, rode in one pulled by cats. There was also the great hunt in which mystic hunters—Odin and the high gods (Aesir) themselves—rode in a great horde over the night sky. The sun and moon were said to be pulled in chariots across the sky while being chased by two wolves, Hati ("hate") and Skoll (loud noise). Odin's horse, Sleipnir, had eight legs. The few times the poetry mentions Sleipnir, he is ridden to the depths of the Norse afterlife/underworld called Hel-heim. H. R. Ellis-Davidson, in her book *The Road to Hel,* suggests these references may be a metaphor for a casket being carried by four pallbearers (i.e., a "horse" with eight legs). Tacitus described ceremonies where a figure of a god was hidden within a cart and driven about a town to give the blessings of fertility.

All of these examples tie into the mystery of travel. There is the element of being able to go from one world to another; we see this element with Sleipnir and Thor's chariot. There are also elements of orderliness and rhythm; these elements are found with the movement of the sun and moon, the positions of which were charted and maintained for secular and religious practice.

Today, we see this rune's energy with the energy of all of our travels. These travels include the daily commute, business travel, and visiting friends and family. There is no better rune than Raido to describe the sacred being present in these actions. Raido has the element of manifestation energy within it. As our lives are sacred prayers, the energy of Raido reflects that. The Norse way was not to sit and be still, but to be up and active. Raido reflects those characteristics with its energy.

KENNAZ

Alternate names: Ken, Kaun, Chaon

Phonetic value: *k*

Translations: *Torch, ulcer, knowing*

Icelandic rune poem:

> *Disease fatal to children*
> *and painful spot*
> *and abode of mortification.*

Anglo-Saxon rune poem:

> *The torch is known to every living man by its pale,*
> * bright flame;*
> *it always burns where princes sit within.*

Norwegian rune poem:

> *Ulcer is fatal to children;*
> *death makes a corpse pale.*

The secret to this rune lies within the Anglo-Saxon rune poem. The word used in this poem is *Ken* (or *Cen*), which translates to "torch." Here we have man-made fire. This fire is not only the one that lights a room where people sit, but also that fire that lights the hearth and forge.

There is a Norse word that best explains the energy of Kennaz: *kenna*, which means "to know." This knowledge is the Nordic presentation of Promethean fire. The "fire of the gods" that Prometheus brought to mankind is the enlightenment of the gods, and so too is the torch of Kennaz. There is scholarly debate about the etymological connection of the word *kenna* and the name of the rune Kennaz.

More pointedly, Kennaz, used in the forge, is a metaphor for the application of knowledge found in Ansuz. We see the smiths of the ages spending years in apprenticeship. Then, as master smiths, they put their knowledge to work. The energy of Kennaz is that of taking what you know and using it.

Some may find difficulty with reconciling the meanings of the Icelandic and Norwegian poems with that of the Anglo-Saxon when it comes to Kennaz. Each of these poems seems to be describing something different. The Icelandic and Norwegian poems tell of a disease or sore spot; the Anglo-Saxon poem tells of a torch with bright flame.

We do know that it is knowledge that ultimately separates childhood from adulthood. As we age, we gain in knowledge and, hopefully, wisdom. Perhaps knowledge is the disease that is fatal to children. Think of those who, for whatever reason, were forced into adulthood at an early age. That change usually happened through some sort of traumatic event in which the child learned of things in the world that usually are best to learn as an adult.

Perhaps Kennaz's connection with ulcers or boils comes from the fever accompanying these conditions. It is with tongue-in-cheek that we can think of a body's high temperature as being "man-made fire."

Today, the usefulness of Kennaz is found in putting to work what you have studied. While many do not work in the field in which they received degrees, they are still applying their knowledge in whatever field they are in. This man-made fire of the new times can be found in not only what you are doing, but also in what you have the potential to do.

Alternate name: Gyfu

Phonetic value: *g*

Translations: *Gift, giving, generosity*

Anglo-Saxon rune poem:

> *Generosity brings credit and honor,*
> *which support one's dignity;*
> *it furnishes help and subsistence*
> *to all broken men who are devoid of aught else.*

Gebo typifies the greatest virtue of the Nordic people: generosity. In the ancient times, homes, farms, and villages were so far apart, it was difficult to reach a destination within a day's travel. So one had to stop at the home of another, possibly a stranger, to spend the night or else face the savage cold of the night. The hospitality and goodwill of a host would have been vital for the traveler's survival.

We might see this virtue of generosity in a verse from the Havamal:

> With Weapons and garments should friends rejoice
> That is visible to one's self
> Great givers and those who give again, are long time
> > friends
> If that which is given, is given well

> With his friends shall a man be a friend
> And gladly give gift for gift
> Laughter with laughter, should one take
> And falsehoods with lies

The Havamal also gives a warning on gift giving:

> Best not to offer, then to blot too often
> A gift expects a return
> Best not to send, then to over sacrifice
> So Thund carved, before the doom of man
> There he rose and came after

The warning is that one should not give too much, because a gift demands a gift. What we can glean from this is something that is common sense found in today's world. It is important to help others, but only when you are in a place to give. If your giving cup is empty, then not only do you have nothing to give others, but also nothing to give to yourself.

Alternate name: Wynn

Phonetic value: *w/v*

Translations: Joy, happiness, win

Anglo-Saxon rune poem:

> *Bliss he enjoys who knows not suffering,*
> *sorrow nor anxiety,*
> *and has prosperity and happiness and a good*
> *enough house.*

Of all the runes, Wunjo is perhaps the easiest one to understand. This is the rune of happiness and joy. As mentioned with Gebo, friendship is found in those who give gift for gift and laughter for laughter. This dynamic exemplifies another Nordic virtue, called *frith*. Frith is the peace and happiness found among friends and family. So sacred was frith that often *frithgards* (peace yards) were established. These were places where weapons combat and aggression were not tolerated. They were often places of sacred worship or law establishment.

Perhaps the best deity that personified this virtue was Baldr. Baldr was the most beautiful and beloved of all the gods. His son was Forseti, who was known for stilling all strife. Wunjo also offers us contrast to the pain and torment of Kennaz. Where there was suffering, there is now peace and joy.

Today, we can look at the energy of Wunjo as leave from our daily toil. If one is in need of an oasis from the rat race, a quick dip in the cool waters of Wunjo eases all ill. Indeed, modern science is showing this to be true. Laughter increases the oxygenation of the blood. It stops the production of cortisol, the stress hormone that is so destructive to the body's immune system. Laughter also promotes the production of endorphins, the body's natural pain relievers. The old adage, "laughter is the best medicine," is proving to be the truth. Laughter is good for the soul as well. It is the highest form of spiritual energy that can exist within a human body. It dispels negative energies and chases away harmful entities.

An alternate name for Wunjo is Wynn. We can think of this name as today's word *win*. It is with success that one can find happiness. Success can take many forms—financial success, success with family and/or friends, success in reaching personal fitness goals, or even a general sense of well-being. To the ancients, success was victory, and pride was taken with each victory. Today, you can look at all of your successes as stepping-stones to winning your ultimate goal. For this, Wunjo can be one of your greatest assets.

Alternate names: Hagall, Haegl

Phonetic value: *h*

Translation: *Hail*

Icelandic rune poem:

> *Cold grain*
> *and shower of sleet*
> *and sickness of serpents.*

Anglo-Saxon rune poem:

> *Hail is the whitest of grain;*
> *it is whirled from the vault of heaven*
> *and is tossed about by gusts of wind*
> *and then it melts into water.*

Norwegian rune poem:

> *Hail is the coldest of grain;*
> *Christ created the world of old.*

The rune poems and all the names for this rune agree as to the nature of Hagalaz. This is the rune of hail. It is the destructive natural force that comes from the storm clouds. There is no way to stop it, and there is little time to prepare for it. Ultimately Hagalaz leads to various levels of destruction or disruption.

To the ancient Nordic people, the energy of the storms was personified by the giants called Jotuns. While a Thurs was a purely destructive giant bent on the abolishment of the gods and mankind (see Thurisaz, ᚦ), a Jotun was a giant of the mountains, the valleys, the skies, and the storms. Jotuns were not evil entities. However, their power and size were seen as destructive to the small worlds humans lived in. Of all of the powers available to the Jotuns, the storms were the most feared.

The hailstorm was one of the most hated storms to the ancients. A strong hailstorm could mean the difference between an easy winter and a difficult one. If the storm destroyed buildings, they would need to be repaired before the coming winter. If the hail destroyed crops before they could be harvested, then there might not be enough grain for the coming winter.

The lessons of all three poems do offer a bit of cryptic hope. They describe hail as the coldest or whitest of grains—an allusion to the fact that hail will melt into water and bring moisture to the soil. A hailstorm is similar to the volcano or forest fire. It is destruction in motion. Once it subsides, life begins to renew itself in the freshly fertile soil, soil that is ripe for growing.

What are the lessons of Hagalaz for today? The first is that there is no way for us to see what may be coming our way. We all surely will face tough times with little to no warning. These situations will range from spilt milk to dramatic, life-altering disruptions. But the second lesson of Hagalaz is that there is always hope. The universe sometimes needs to clear space to let new things grow. The universe abhors a vacuum. In order for us to get something new in our lives, we may have to clear away the old. Hagalaz provides the energy to clear away stagnated and hindering processes in favor of forward-moving progress.

NAUTHIZ

Alternate names: Nied, Nauth, Nyd

Phonetic value: *n*

Translations: *Need, necessity, constraint*

Icelandic rune poem:

> *Grief of the bond-maid*
> *and state of oppression*
> *and toilsome work.*

Anglo-Saxon rune poem:

> *Trouble is oppressive to the heart;*
> *yet often it proves a source of help and salvation*
> *to the children of men, to everyone who heeds it*
> > *betimes.*

Norwegian rune poem:

> *Constraint gives scant choice;*
> *a naked man is chilled by the frost.*

Nauthiz is that energy that has been a constant companion of all living things from time immemorial. All living things have needs that form the basis of life, such as acquiring food, water, and shelter and maintaining health. The energy of Nauthiz is that of necessity. It is not the energy of want or desire, but the need for that which is vital for survival and a thriving life.

The names of this rune have changed very little through the ages. They are all cognates of the word *Nied*. As time marched on, *Nied* gave way to the modern English word *need*. Tied in with this concept are the ideas of constraint, grief, and trouble.

The Icelandic and Norwegian poems refer to Nauthiz as the grief of the bond-maid (servant) and as giving little choice. Those in the lowest class of society, called thralls, had to do toilsome work for little to no pay or recognition. Yet their backbreaking labor was vital to the livelihood of the ancient Nordic community. People who suffer a life of hard work are rightly referred to as the salt of the earth. If it were not for their efforts, all of society would crumble.

The lessons of the modern psychologist Abraham Maslow tie in well here. Maslow says that only when our needs for sustenance, shelter, and a place in society have been satiated do we have the ability to foster our spiritual side. Even the monasteries, where the denizens swore themselves to a life of poverty while pursuing spiritual matters, had this principle covered. The residents toiled in the day to plant and harvest crops. They lived in shelter, and all of their basic necessities were provided for. Having their basic needs met offered them ample opportunity to engage in their spiritual practices.

When we have the burden of need hanging over our heads, we can do little else but work to satiate that need. This is the meaning of the "source of help and salvation" mentioned in the Anglo-Saxon poem. When a need arises within our lives, we must work to resolve it. If we choose to ignore it in favor of spiritual or material gain, we only do ourselves a disservice.

Alternate name: Is

Phonetic value: *i*

Translation: *Ice*

Icelandic rune poem:

> *Bark of rivers*
> *and roof of the wave*
> *and destruction of the doomed.*

Anglo-Saxon rune poem:

> *Ice is very cold and immeasurably slippery;*
> *it glistens as clear as glass and most like to gems;*
> *it is a floor wrought by the frost, fair to look upon.*

Norwegian rune poem:

> *Ice we call the broad bridge;*
> *the blind man must be led.*

There are two forces that shaped the world known as Midgardh (our physical universe): fire and ice. Ice was the most primal and stagnant force known to the ancients. Where Hagalaz was the ice (hail) of the whirring, destructive storm, Isa was the static, non-moving, solid block of water.

In the lands of the North, ice covered a good portion of the landscape year-round. In Iceland and Greenland, the vast numbers of glaciers were commonplace in the lore and in daily life. In many ways, we can relate today to the way the ancients saw ice. We gasp in awe of brilliant landscapes covered in snow. We stand agape at great waterfalls that have frozen into giant columns. We take pleasure in gliding effortlessly over the surface of a smoothly frozen lake.

We also share the same trepidation and respect that the ancients had for the ice. We know that being caught in the ice will mean certain death. Hence, ice is the "destruction of the doomed." Calling ice "the roof of the wave" is an all-too-knowing understanding of the dangers of being caught under the ice. It also alludes to the many treacheries that are inherent in ice. One may fall on slippery ice, one could fall through thin ice, or the ice may be so vast and treacherous that it is impassable. There is a line in the Havamal that suggests we praise ice only after it has been crossed. Perhaps the warning here is the same as the modern adage of not counting your chickens until they have hatched.

Today, the lesson of Isa tells us that all things can slow or even stop. This slowing or stopping may be a good or bad thing. We may feel the need to constantly be working and productive. But if there is no rest, even machines will fail. The energy of Isa can help us to slow a hailstorm (again Hagalaz, ᚺ) in life. As we run in the rat race, it is growing increasingly difficult to keep up with the quickly changing times. Yet if we don't take a moment to "smell the roses," they may be gone. The energy of Isa can help us do this.

JERA

Alternate names: Jara, Ar, Ger

Phonetic value: *j/y*

Translations: *Year, harvest, boon*

Icelandic rune poem:

> *Boon to men*
> *and good summer*
> *and thriving crops.*

Anglo-Saxon rune poem:

> *Summer is a joy to men, when God, the holy*
> *King of Heaven,*
> *suffers the earth to bring forth shining fruits*
> *for rich and poor alike.*

Norwegian rune poem:

> *Plenty is a boon to men;*
> *I say that Frodi was generous.*

Jera is a rune of boon and plenty. This name is the origin to the modern word *year*. To the ancients, it represented the notion of harvest. It was the boon and good summer. It represented a completion of the year's tasks. If a summer had been bad and yielded little harvest, there might not be enough food for all to survive the winter. The same would be true if famine had struck the livestock.

When winter came to settle in the northern lands, all agricultural activities stopped. Animals that would not be able to survive the cold were slaughtered. The harvest of grains and fish was brought in and stored. During these dark months of winter, the benefits of the previous months' work became vital to survival. The villages were often cut off from each other in the winter months. The roads were frozen over with ice, and there were scant hours of sunlight to light the way for travelers. There was simply very little chance for a farm to receive aid if food became tight in the dark winter months. For this reason, Jera must have been a highly revered rune. It meant the survival of the family and farm for another year.

In the modern world, we have the benefits of instant communication, easy winter travel (compared to a thousand years ago), and supermarkets. All of these benefits disconnect us from what the ancient people had to endure. But they do not mean we are disconnected from the energies of Jera. These energies are just as alive and well today as they were more than a thousand years ago.

Today, the power of Jera is found in the results of the work we do. The ancient people labored through the short growing season, pushing their way through the harvest to stockpile their goods for the coming winter. All of this hard work led up to their reward—the bountiful harvest. Today Jera is still the boon that comes from our endeavors; Jera is our success.

Compare Jera to Fehu and Gebo. Where Fehu is a payment you put into something, Jera is a goal you have gained. Where Gebo is a gift that is granted and a gain that is expected from the gift, Jera is what you have worked hard for and now get to keep. Jera reminds us that there is a reward for effort well spent. You get out of your effort only as much as you have put in.

EIHWAZ

Alternate names: Yr, Eoh

Phonetic value: *ei*

Translation: *Yew tree*

Icelandic rune poem:

> *Bent bow*
> *and brittle iron*
> *and giant of the arrow.*

Anglo-Saxon rune poem:

> *The yew is a tree with rough bark,*
> *hard and fast in the earth, supported by its roots,*
> *a guardian of flame and a joy upon an estate.*

Norwegian rune poem:

> *Yew is the greenest of trees in winter;*
> *it singes when it burns.*

Eihwaz is one of the more difficult runes for us to understand in the modern world. To the ancients, Eihwaz literally was the yew tree. To understand what this tree meant to them, we need to piece together the bits and pieces about the yew tree from lore and mythology.

The poems refer to the yew being best for making bows. Indeed, many archers preferred yew as a superior wood, due to its hardness and flexibility. This aspect of the yew is what is referred to in the Icelandic poem. The Anglo-Saxon poem describes the tree's outward physical characteristics, but never explains why it is, as the poem says, "a joy on the estate." The Norwegian poem gives a clue to the meaning of the elusive Anglo-Saxon line when it says "yew is the greenest of trees in winter." The yew, an evergreen, produces berries only in the deepest of winter. The last line of the Norwegian poem, "sing(e)ing when it burns," indicates that singeing is considered an auspicious and a magically loaded event.

Yew does have a darker side. It may be the most poisonous tree in the world. It is said that sitting under a yew tree during a hot summer day will first produce visions, then death. The yew tree was, and still is, a very common tree in graveyards. For these reasons, the yew tree is considered a tree of death. Norse headstones typically bore two runes from the Younger Futhark: ᛉ (Mann) is used for the date of birth and ᛦ (Yr) for the date of death. Yr is the Younger Futhark version of Eihwaz. It has a different phonetic value, but retains the same meaning.

There is debate as to whether Yggdrasil, the world tree, was a yew or an ash. Yggdrasil is that force that holds all nine of the worlds of Norse cosmology in place. To travel along this tree, one must leave his or her body. Thus, Yggdrasil is the conduit for Nordic shamanic travel—a supernatural or even deathlike state of existence.

In modern times the yew tree can certainly still reflect aspects of death. Sometimes it is the death of the body that leads to the birth of spiritual existence. We do not need to die in order to connect our selves to all the worlds around us. Eihwaz can be seen as the conduit by which we are connected to the lower, middle, and upper worlds, that is, all the realms of all the realities. This force connects to these planes simultaneously. It reminds us that we are never far from our spiritual origins and that we walk with death, in all of its mysterious forms, in every moment of our lives.

PERTHRO

Alternate names: Perth, Peordh

Phonetic value: *p*

Translations: *Dice cup, fate, unknown*

Anglo-Saxon rune poem:

> *Peorth is a source of recreation and amusement*
> *to the great,*
> *where warriors sit blithely together in the*
> *banqueting-hall*

Perthro is the most mysterious of all of the runes. No historian, translator, or literary expert has come up with a satisfactory translation of its name. It has been suggested to mean everything from "dice cup" to "birth room" (a womb?) to "fate." The best explanation for *Perthro* is that it is a nonsense word. The reason for this pseudo-definition becomes clear with a deeper understanding of the fatalism in which the ancient Nordic people believed.

They believed that their entire lives were plotted out from the moment of birth. Everyone is set on a path that will conclude just as preordained. This concept is called one's *orlog*. Today, we may call this destiny. Along this path of destiny, one has the ability to choose how he or she walks, runs, or does anything else. Ultimately, one always has the choice of whether to act nobly or ignobly. How one lives his or her life determines how that life plays out.

And along this path, one never travels alone. One always has an assortment of guides helping him or her through various deviations along this path. The ancient Norse called the beings the Disir. They quite often were deceased female ancestors who took an active interest in the daily workings of one's life.

The concept of Perthro is the fact that we never really know what is about to happen, but we do have the choice of what to do in the moment. This concept is what led some to equate Perthro with a dice cup and luck. One can choose to pick up the cup and roll the dice, but that person cannot choose how the dice land. The probability of the dice coming out in a person's favor relies on all of the many fatalistic concepts the ancient Norse knew so well. If one acted nobly, then there was a higher chance of the dice roll being favorable.

Today, Perthro means that we are all still tied into the grand web of fate that the Norns—the weavers/carvers of fate—have made. We all are born with our destinies to fulfill. The effects of fate, the Norns, and the Disir, play upon us just as strongly as our actions and intentions. In essence, we become our own greatest Norn. We are at the hands of fate just as much as we *are* the hands of fate. The energy of Perthro is always with us, guiding and directing our lives. Perthro has this simple, yet strange effect on all things.

Alternate names: Algiz, Eolh

Phonetic value: *z*

Translations: *Elk, elk sedge*

Anglo-Saxon rune poem:

> *The Eolh-sedge is mostly to be found in a marsh;*
> *it grows in the water and makes a ghastly wound,*
> *covering with blood every warrior who touches it.*

Elhaz follows the enigmatic flow of the two runes before it, Eihwaz (ᛇ) and Perthro (ᛈ). Its nature is deeply spiritual, yet mysterious. The literal definition of this rune refers to the elk. The ancient Norse had a plethora of animals to which they prescribed magical attributes. The elk had the power of strength, stamina, and a spiritual protectiveness attributed to it.

The Anglo-Saxons took the concept one step further and applied it to elk sedge, a plant the elk were fond of eating. Elk sedge is a barbed plant that grows in swampy territories. If one were to grab the plant and pull it up, that person's hand would suffer a "ghastly wound." There are tales of people escaping pursuers by hiding in swamps surrounded by elk sedge. It is a bit of a stretch to attach the nature of grasping elk sedge with the protective nature of Elhaz. The emphasis of this comparison is to show the passive protective nature of Elhaz whether it is surrounding a swamp, home, or person.

If we look at the shape of Elhaz, we certainly can imagine a stag with horns upon its head. Further reflection may show that it is a diagram of a flow of energy from the realms of the gods and elves to the world of man. A very early runic shape was formed from a combination of Yr (λ) and Elhaz (Υ). We could use this combination shape as a rudimentary diagram of the nine worlds.

We could use this combination shape as a rudimentary diagram of seven of the nine worlds in Norse cosmology.

Upper Worlds:

> Asgardh – realm of the gods
> Vanaheim – realm of the fertility/nature gods
> Ljosalfheim – realm of the light elves/Disir

Middle World:

> Midgardh – realm of mankind

Lower Worlds:

> Helheim – underworld of the dead
> Svartalfheim – realm of the dark elves/dwarves
> Jotunheim – realm of giants

There are two primal worlds not represented in this diagram: Muspellsheim, the primal world of fire, and Niflheim, the primal world of ice and mist.

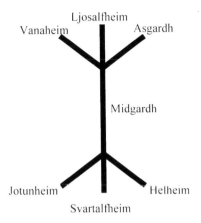

Ljosalfheim

Vanaheim   Asgardh

Midgardh

Jotunheim   Helheim

Svartalfheim

The combination of Elhaz (ᛉ) and Yr (ᛦ) forms a shape representing
a placement of seven of the nine worlds of Norse cosmology.

From this diagram, we can see that the upper three worlds connect with Midgardh (our physical universe) via the shape of Elhaz. This connection means the upper-world energy flows into our realm via this rune. Therefore, people using this rune would become conduits of this energy of the upper three worlds. They bring the energy of the gods and light elves into their immediate surroundings. This energy is distasteful, if not poisonous, to the destructive energies of the beings that reside within the lower worlds. This energy dispels darkness and disperses all harmful energies. Simply put, Elhaz is the rune of protection and invocation of all higher-level energies.

SOWILO

Alternate names: Sol, Sigel

Phonetic value: *s*

Translation: *Sun*

Icelandic rune poem:

> *Shield of the clouds*
> *and shining ray*
> *and destroyer of ice.*

Anglo-Saxon rune poem:

> *The sun is ever a joy in the hopes of seafarers*
> *when they journey away over the fishes' bath,*
> *until the courser of the deep bears them to land.*

Norwegian rune poem:

> *Sun is the light of the world;*
> *I bow to the divine decree.*

The literal definition of Sowilo is easy to grasp. It is "the sun." From its name, Sol, another name we still call the sun, we have the root of the word *solar*. The ancient Scandinavians were not sun worshipers, but they did highly revere and honor the sun. Unlike many traditions of the world, the Norse considered the sun to be a female being. They called her Sunna. The sun was of female energy for, like women, it nurtured life. Sunna was drawn around the world in a chariot pulled by two horses, whose names meant Early-waker and All-swift. She was chased by a wolf named Skoll. It is said that the wolf catching and devouring Sunna is a precursor to Ragnarok, the battle that brings about the end of the world.

The Norse held great festivals for the sun. The most noted are the rites of Yule. Yule comes in the dead of winter, at the time of the solstice—when, in the northern lands, the sun does not rise for one full day. During this time, as many lights as possible were lit, and a log was burned the whole night through to hold vigil for the return of the sun. For if the sun did not return, it meant that the great winter was upon them. This great winter, lasting four years, was the first sign of the coming of Ragnarok.

There is a contrast here between Sowilo with Kennaz. While Kennaz was manmade fire used for making things, Sowilo represents natural and supernatural fire. The ancients saw the sun as not just a nurturing force; it had a destructive side as well. The sun was the only thing that could destroy icebergs. We still feel its energy in the hot summer months. We can imagine that it was for this reason that the ancients decided to give Sowilo the shape of a lightning bolt ($\mathsf{5}$). This shape is still seen today in the English letter s.

Tying these aspects together is the fact that the sun was the bane of giants and trolls. The lore shows us that these subterranean beings turned to stone when sun hit them. These beings are also great enemies of Thor, the thunderer, giving us another connection with the lightning bolt image and the sun. Both can be a harsh, directed force.

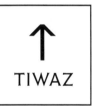

Alternate names: Tyr, Tiw, Tiu

Phonetic value: *t*

Translations: *Tyr*

Icelandic rune poem:

> *God with one hand*
> *and leavings of the wolf*
> *and prince of temples.*

Anglo-Saxon rune poem:

> Tiw is a guiding star; well does it keep faith
>   with princes;
> it is ever on its course over the mists of night and
>   never fails.

Norwegian rune poem:

> Tyr is a one-handed god;
> often has the smith to blow.

The energy of the rune Tiwaz is best explained by the legend of Tyr. The gods had found themselves raising a young wolf pup. As this wolf grew, it became huge, and its hunger became insatiable. This wolf came to be destructive and far too powerful for any of the gods to control. For this reason the gods asked the dark elves, the master smiths, to fashion an unbreakable fetter. To bind this wolf, the gods created a game. They asked the wolf to break various chains—a task he accomplished with ease. Then the gods brought out their bond; it looked like a thin ribbon. The wolf became suspicious and only agreed to try and break it if one of the gods would put his hand into the wolf's mouth. All of the gods shied away from this challenge, except one. Tyr placed his hand into the mouth of the wolf so the beast could be bound. Once the great wolf discovered the deception, he severed Tyr's hand.

This parable of how Tyr lost his hand is a tale of self-sacrifice for the greater good. The wolf represents pure, untamable, chaotic destruction. Tyr is the embodiment of the noble deeds one must do if the chaos is to be stopped. For this reason, Tyr was often called on by the Norse warrior class. There are numerous Norse artifacts of warfare that bear the Tiwaz (↑) rune. There is even a passage in the Havamal that suggests one should chant the charm of the Tyr rune under a shield. The Sigrdrifumal also talks of calling upon Tyr for protection in battle.

The sense of duty and discipline is the essence of any warrior class. Look no further than the U.S. military of today. It is a strongly hierarchal system. Every moment of every day is deliberately planned out. We can look at the uniforms, routines of marching, the paperwork, and the flow of orders. This structure is all the work of the Tyr rune.

Today, the energy of Tyr, through the Tiwaz (↑) rune, will help one follow the straight and narrow. It will help one stay on task, focused, and, all in all, disciplined. The discipline of Tyr is not of punishment or self-torture. It is the discipline of following a set route, a planned pattern, and noble actions.

BERKANA

Alternate names: Bjarken, Beorc, Brica

Phonetic value: *b*

Translation: *Birch tree*

Icelandic rune poem:

> *Leafy twig*
> *and little tree*
> *and fresh young shrub.*

Anglo-Saxon rune poem:

> *The poplar bears no fruit; yet without seed it brings*
>   *forth suckers,*
> *for it is generated from its leaves.*
> *Splendid are its branches and gloriously adorned*
> *its lofty crown which reaches to the skies.*

Norwegian rune poem:

> *Birch has the greenest leaves of any shrub;*
> *Loki was fortunate in his deceit.*

Quite often Tiwaz is viewed as a rune of nonfertile masculine energy. Berkana is the antithesis; it represents fertile female energy. The shape of Berkana is often thought to resemble a side view of the breasts and belly of a pregnant mother.

We can see that all of the poems refer to a type of tree. *Berkana* literally means the birch tree. In Norse society it was, and still is, a common practice for couples to beat each other with birch twigs. We see this custom during wedding ceremonies and rites of spring. Through this action, the couple blesses each other with the fertility that Berkana would represent.

This energy would easily apply to any of the fertility goddesses of Norse lore. Freya's energy fits Berkana well, as she was the goddess who often is associated with carnal desires. Frigg, Odin's wife, was the mother of the family. Gefjon was known for plowing free the lands that became the Danish island of Zealand. She was the caretaker of virgins or children who died.

Today, Berkana represents any sort of opportunity. We can think of the energy of Berkana as being a wide-open, fertile field. Into this field, seeds must be planted. These seeds may be ideas, plans, visions of the future, or dreams. And each of these seeds needs an appropriate field to be planted in—a womb to grow in. Berkana can mean different things to different people. To a stockbroker it could be a bull market. To a musician it could be the fans. To a student working on her degree it could be the field she is studying. Her efforts and educational goals become the seed.

Berkana also has the energies of female fertility and female health. It is a very appropriate rune to use to promote the fertility of a woman's womb. Its nature also represents the nurturing, giving, and caring aspects of motherhood. Quite often, you will find Berkana called the mother rune. (Not that it is the mother of all runes; rather, it is the rune of mothers.) Some suggest this rune is appropriate to paint on a mother in labor. Others keep it around as a symbol of their nurturing and caregiving nature.

EHWAZ

Alternate name: Eh

Phonetic value: *e*

Translation: *Horse*

Anglo-Saxon rune poem:

> *The horse is a joy to princes in the presence of warriors.*
> *A steed in the pride of its hoofs,*
> *when rich men on horseback bandy words about it;*
> *and it is ever a source of comfort to the restless.*

Ehwaz has a phonetic value of *e*. Its name literally means "horse," and its shape suggests a horse standing in profile. The Anglo-Saxon rune poem describes the horse as being valuable to princes when among warriors. The horse described is not just any horse but a prideful and powerful one, the type used for battle or for stately affairs.

Therefore, the energy represented by Ehwaz reflects status and power. It is an assumed tenet of the Norse tradition that one must always seek to increase his or her might and main—that is, the waxing of influence and affluence. To the ancient Nordic people, the horse was a symbol of a person's stature. The bigger and more powerful the horse a person had, the greater his stature.

There is an otherworldly approach to the meaning of the horse. Traditional Norse burial ceremonies always had a theme of travel. Poor people were buried with a strong pair of shoes to help them on their long journey. There are graves of women buried with carts. These women may have been respected as mystical leaders or priestesses. There are the ever-famous ship burials of kings. People of great status, but who were not quite kings, were buried with their horses. We also have Odin's horse, Sleipnir. The major mentions of Sleipnir in the literature speak of journeys to Helheim, the land of the dead, by Odin and Hermod, a messenger of Odin.

Today, one of the most prominent status symbols is the automobile, the modern equivalent of the horse. But to truly be the equivalent of the ancient Norse horse, the car would have to be flashy, powerful, quick, and very expensive—a sports or luxury car, for example.

Metaphysically, the symbol of the horse is useful for those who wish to travel to the spiritual realms. In shamanic journeying, a horse makes a useful guide. It is swift, powerful, and, as the old song goes, it knows the way.

Alternate names: Mann, Madhr

Phonetic value: *m*

Translations: *Man, mankind*

Icelandic rune poem:

> *Delight of man*
> *and augmentation of the earth*
> *and adorner of ships.*

Anglo-Saxon rune poem:

> *The joyous man is dear to his kinsmen;*
> *yet every man is doomed to fail his fellow,*
> *since the Lord by his decree will commit the vile*
> *carrion to the earth.*

Norwegian rune poem:

> *Man is an augmentation of the dust;*
> *great is the claw of the hawk.*

Mannaz is the *m* rune, both in shape and phonetic value. Some have said it is the shape of two people kissing or hugging. Nevertheless, the meaning of the energy of Mannaz is as its name suggests: man, in both in the singular and the plural senses.

In ancient rune carvings, shortcuts were occasionally used. If a rune's name or alternate name was needed for a phrase, a single rune was used in place of the word. Thus, Mannaz (ᛗ) was used for the word *man*. This rune was used to represent the individual, as in "a bold man," or in the plural for mankind.

It is this latter definition that is suggested in the poems, as all three refer to mankind. In the Icelandic and Norwegian poems, the phrase "augmentation of the dust" and "augmentation of the earth" are references to the biblical phrase "dust to dust."

Today, we can use the energy of Mannaz as a modifier of runic energy. When Mannaz shows up in rune readings, it often indicates that the associated runes are directly connected to the person the reading is for. When doing active rune work, Mannaz directs the energies of the accompanying runes straight into the person for whom the runes were carved and loaded.

We can think of Mannaz energy as self-centered but not to a destructive point. If one is to be useful and helpful to others, he or she must be sure he or she is taken care of first. If you want to fill the cups of others, you must be sure yours is full first. This is the subtle lesson of Mannaz: you must always take care of yourself first. You must apply a bit of controlled selfishness. Once you are certain that you are healthy and strong, then you can help others. If you have nothing, you can give only nothing. This principle is directly tied in with increasing might and main. The ancients prided themselves on their generosity and hospitality, but only when they had it to give. They always strove to be able to provide more, so that their communities could not only survive, but also thrive.

LAGUZ

Alternate names: Lagu, Logr

Phonetic value: *l*

Translations: *Lake, water, ocean*

Icelandic rune poem:

> *Eddying stream*
> *and broad geyser*
> *and land of the fish.*

Anglo-Saxon rune poem:

> *The ocean seems interminable to men,*
> *if they venture on the rolling bark*
> *and the waves of the sea terrify them*
> *and the courser of the deep heed not its bridle.*

Norwegian rune poem:

> *A waterfall is a River which falls from a mountain-side;*
> *but ornaments are of gold.*

Laguz, simply stated, is a water rune. It represents everything from a stream, river, or lake to an ocean. Its name, though not etymologically connected, is similar to the English word *lagoon*. It has the phonetic value of *l*. The shape of Laguz suggests a broken reed on the shore of a lake or stream. It may even be a leek hanging from a beaker of beer.

In the Norse traditions there are a great many legends associated with every type of naturally occurring water. There are the rivers that flow from the great well Hvergelmir, and from these rivers flow all waters and all living things. There are the springs and the mysterious creatures that inhabit them. Odin won great wisdom when he was able to drink from the well of Mimir. He sacrificed his eye to the well but gained the knowledge of the fates of all things. It was from this deed he gained the name *Grim*.

Tied to the myths of the oceans are great creatures such as Jormungand, the great serpent that wrapped itself all the way around the world. At the coming of Ragnarok, Thor falls to Jormungand just as Thor kills him. Associated with the ocean are certain gods, sometimes thought of as Jotuns. There is Aegir, the great beer brewer of the gods, and his wife, Ran. They are the keepers of the deep ocean. Of the shallow seas we find Njord, the granter of great riches.

We can see there are many mysteries associated with water. Laguz represents the deeper unknown and mystical forces that we share the world with. Today, we still attribute this sense of mystery and emotion to the water element. Those who do elemental workings know that water is the element of emotions, the subconscious, and psychic workings. (These same qualities are tied in with lunar forces.) Laguz can be used with other runes to help one in psychic matters, with dreams, or to heal emotions. When paired with Elhaz (ᛉ), it makes an excellent runic combination for Seidh working or shamanic journeying.

Alternate names: Ingwaz, Ing

Phonetic value: *ng*

Translations: *Ing, Freyr*

Anglo-Saxon rune poem:

> *Ing was first seen by men among the East-Danes,*
> *till, followed by his chariot,*
> *he departed eastwards over the waves.*
> *So the Heardingas named the hero.*

With Inguz, the Icelandic and Norwegian poems leave us. The only explanation of Inguz comes from the Anglo-Saxon rune poem. The phonetic value is *ng*, a sound found in words ending in *ing*. Words such as *Viking*, which means "of the wik," or *Aetheling*, which means "of the Aethel," are examples of Nordic words with the ending of ◇ (*ing*).

Another such word is *Ingling*, meaning, people who are the descendents of Ing—the people of Sweden. The most honored god of these people was Freyr. The ruling class of Sweden owed its lineage to the god Freyr. It must be noted that *Freyr* is just a title that literally translates to "lord." The name most often given to the god Freyr is *Ing* or *Ingvar*.

Inguz is the rune of Freyr and all of his associated energies. The statues of Freyr show him with a large phallus, so it is reasonable to assume that Freyr represented the fertile male energies.

Also, Freyr was the twin brother to Freya. Since she was representative of the fertile woman, again, it is safe to assume that Freyr represents the fertile male. The shape of Inguz suggests it might be a seed—the seed that needs to be planted in the fertile soil of Berkana. Freyr and Freya are members of the Vanir, the race of fertility gods. In addition to overseeing agrarian matters, they were also the givers of wealth. Many prayers to Freyr were for wealth and peace.

Thus we have an effective modern use of this rune. There will always be a need for growth and expansion, which is the basis for life and the development and sustaining of that life. The key term here is "to sustain." As long as we humans need our connection to nature, we will always need Freyr's influence. He does not represent the destructive, selfish attitudes that have come about over the ages. Instead, Freyr will continue to promote life and its increasing affluence.

For this reason the energies of Inguz cannot be used for wholly selfish means. Yes, one can use its seedling energies to get something he or she needs or wants, but not if it is destructive. Since Inguz is the seed, it represents the spark of ideas, notions, and creativity. Alone, a seed can only sit and wait to release its potential energies. But once it is placed within a medium appropriate to its nature, then it will grow, thrive, and reproduce.

DAGAZ

Alternate names: Dag, Daeg

Phonetic value: *d*

Translation: *Day*

Anglo-Saxon rune poem:

> *Day, the glorious light of the Creator, is sent by the Lord;*
> *it is beloved of men, a source of hope and happiness to*
> *rich and poor,*
> *and of service to all.*

Dagaz is the rune of day. It has the phonetic value of *d*. Sometimes it is associated with the modern Icelandic letter of *eth*. Where Thurisaz has the same phonetic value as the *th* in *theme*, Dagaz's value is that of the *d* in day or *th* as in *father*. The word *Dagaz* evolved into *Dag* and *Daeg*. Eventually, the hard *g* became a softer *y* sound, turning *Dag/Daeg* into the modern word *day*.

There may be a connection with the Daguz (ᛞ) rune and a stanza from the Havamal. In the rune charms section of the Havamal, one of the charms refers to Delling's doorstep. Delling is a dark elf who was the father of Dag, who rides the chariot of the sun over the course of the daytime. Dag, the day, is a constant companion to Sunna, the sun. (It must be noted that the word *delling* translates to "dawn.")

Many of the modern sources describing runes say Dagaz is a rune of transformation. It is the light of the day that ends a cycle of time. The ancient Norse kept calendar days by the moon, reckoning their days as the passage of night. The coming of dawn and day represented the change of calendar day.

All of these details lead to Dagaz's transformation energy. It is the energy of the 180-degree turn. The energy represented by the tarot card Death is the same for Dagaz—that is, a complete life transformation, literally from night into day. Dagaz is the energy of the rising sun at daybreak. It is the transformation from dark into light.

Today this energy has great uses as a changer of ways. This rune represents a change from night into day. It is not the changes that come from year to year or life to life. Instead, it is step-by-step transformation. If one is looking to transform his or her life, such as by losing weight, earning more money, or learning a new skill, the changes must not be made all at once. If one loses a lot of weight quickly, he or she tends to gain it back because the person hasn't really made a lifestyle change. This lifestyle change can only come one day at time.

Alternate name: Ethel

Phonetic value: *o*

Translations: *Inheritance, legacy, estate*

Anglo-Saxon rune poem:

> *An estate is very dear to every man,*
> *if he can enjoy there in his house*
> *whatever is right and proper in constant prosperity.*

Othala and Dagaz are often found changing places in various carvings of the Elder Futhark. In fact, scholars debate on which rune is the most appropriate to end the Futhark. For the workings we are about to undertake, we will use Othala as the final rune.

The phonetic value of Othala is *o*. There seems to be no agreed upon reason for the shape of the rune. The energy of Othala is that of the law of Othal. The Anglo-Saxon rune poem refers to this law as "an estate [that] is dear to every man."

When a leader of an estate died, the custom was to have an othal stone erected in his honor. These stones would state who raised the stone and for whom. This information was essential to the ancient Norse. It is written that when a man died, his estate was divided into thirds. One third was buried with him, one third was used for his funeral, the last third was given to his direct descendent. This direct descendent was usually the first-born son, who was also the one who paid to raise the stone. The land tied to the estate was also given to the first-born son. Thus, the othal stone informed visitors that the old owner was dead and let them know who the new owner was.

The energy of Othala is that of inheritance and legacies. It represents our ancestors and what we have gained from them. At the very least, we have the genetic code they passed on, the culture we live in, and their stories.

Othala contrasts very nicely with Fehu. Where Fehu represents the medium of exchange, Othala represents nontransferable wealth—at least, wealth that is not easily transferable. This argument is one that upholds Othala's place at the end of the Futhark. Fehu begins the Futhark with the notion of payments; Othala ends the Futhark with the notion of wealth gained from tradition.

Exercise 2: Getting to Know the Runes

To truly understand the runes, you must know them for yourself. Much of what has been written about them is from the viewpoint of the ancients. Interjected throughout modern books are the viewpoints of the various authors, who seek to communicate the essence of the runes to the reader through a physical medium. But the actual nature of the runes is not physical, and therefore cannot be truly understood by physical means. You need to undertake a personal process to gain a deeper level of understanding of the essential energy of the runes.

I would recommend you obtain as many viewpoints of the runes as possible. Try reading books on runes by various authors. They will all give their views of the runes as well as different historical and literary points. None of the authors are wrong, but you may find some contradictory views. Some of these views may even clash with yours. If so, then you are making great progress with understanding runes.

Subconscious Observations

When you feel you have a fairly general knowledge of the runes, then it is time for you to discover them with your own understanding by exploring their basic nature. To do this, you will need to enter a sacred inner space found with meditation.

Success in this meditation is facilitated through preparedness. Have the pages to the Runic Meditation Log in the following pages open and ready to write on. Set up the intention of this meditation for exploring a maximum of three runes at a time. Read up on these three runes. Have their shapes, names, and functions memorized, as you will need to recall this information with your eyes closed. Also, turn off the phone, close the door, and let everyone know that you need the next several minutes to yourself.

The first step is to set up sacred space. If you have a process that you have already established and are comfortable with, then by all means follow it. A simple means of setting sacred space is to simply light a candle or some incense. This act tells your subconscious that the room and setting you are in now is a space set aside from the normal world. The more you perform this process, the easier and quicker it will be to pull yourself out of the ordinary everyday world.

The next step is to find a resting position that will be comfortable for several minutes. For some, this position will be sitting, for others it may be laying down. If you lie down and find yourself falling asleep, sit up. Conversely, if you sit up and are having difficulty relaxing, you may benefit from lying down.

Once you find yourself reasonably relaxed, take three deep breaths. The way you breathe is important. Breathing from the chest will cause you to be alert and active. Breathing deeply, from the belly, will help you relax and tune out your conscious mind. This belly breath follows a special rhythm. The inhale needs to be half as long as the exhale; for example, you might inhale for a count of five, then exhale to a count of ten. This rhythm is the pace of breathing while you are asleep. By breathing from the belly and following the half in/twice out rhythm, your body will switch, automatically and easily, into a deeply relaxed state. (A side benefit to this breathing technique is stress management. During the course of your day, if you find yourself stressed, doing this simple breathing pattern will dramatically reduce your tension. It will help restore your vital physical, mental, emotional, and spiritual functions.)

After three breaths, you should be quite relaxed, and you may notice your focus drifting away from your breathing. If so, that is good. It means your mind is now ready to begin.

Before starting with your runic explorations, you need to make an agreement with your conscious mind. The conscious mind can be like a spoiled child. It needs to develop discipline through repetition and positive reinforcement. It also needs acknowledgment that it is important. If these things do not happen, it will constantly enter into your meditation space and distract you from your work.

First, accept that with your first few attempts at this exercise, your conscious mind may drift in. That is OK. When you find your thoughts drifting away from the runes, especially to everyday subjects, acknowledge the thoughts. Tell yourself that the thought is important and that you will work with it at a later time. Tell yourself that right now you are exploring the runes, and when you are done, you will be calm, rested, and ready to give your full attention to the matter. Do this every time the stray thoughts come up, then return your focus to the work at hand. You will notice, very quickly, the amount of stray thoughts will dwindle and disappear, leaving you open to focus all of your attention to the runes.

To focus on the runes, always start with a breath. Breathe in, and upon exhaling, state the name of the rune aloud. While you give the name, remember what the shape of the rune is. Say the name of the rune three times. Each time, imagine yourself getting deeper and deeper into the rune.

Start noticing what is happening. What do you feel? Are there any particular emotions that come up? Do you notice any color, texture, scent, or sound? What other images pop up?

Ask yourself what word or short phrase best describes what you are experiencing. Make a mental note of that word or phrase. Now explore what that word means to you. For example, the phrase for Fehu might come as "medium of exchange." To you, this concept could mean money, the stock exchange, bills, or payments. It could mean capital or hard work. The next question is what sort of things can be exchanged and how.

Once you have this basic understanding, open your eyes and write down your impressions in your Rune Meditation Log. Your mind will stay in its subconscious state for the moment it takes to do so, but the information can begin to drift away, so write quickly.

Once you have written down the information, sit back or lie down. Before closing your eyes again, you may look at the shape, name, and meaning of the next rune you are going to work with. When you close your eyes, take three deep breaths, and you will be back in that same deep state of relaxation. You will be ready to explore the next rune.

Once you have completed your exploration of your three chosen runes, take a few deep breaths from the chest. This type of breathing will tell your body it is time to become alert and active again. Tell your conscious mind that the time has come for you to return your attention to it.

The more you do this meditation process, the easier it gets and the deeper the understanding you will receive. You will also notice you will be more relaxed in your daily life, you will sleep better, and you may find a deeper spiritual connection with your daily life. A side benefit is stress reduction and the healing that comes to the body when stress is reduced.

Conscious Observations

After you have completed your subconscious exploration of the runes and logged your observations, it will be time to consciously explore them. Try to determine what you learned in your meditation and what this information might mean to the you and You aspects of your life. Each rune has an energy that can be understood by all, but only you have the key to understanding it deeply for yourself.

It is important to note that the subconscious and conscious levels of understanding the runes really are two different things. The subconscious observation ties you with your emotional and spiritual connection to the runes. The subconscious is that part of you that does not think or make connections with words. It only uses the basic, uninterpreted information from your senses.

The conscious observation process comes from that part of you that does use words. These words form the intellectual understanding of the runic energy. In conscious observation, it is OK to interpret, but not to judge, what was received by your subconscious portion of the exploration.

There may be different views coming in from different parts of your psyche. This is OK. By finding the common ground within these different views, you will discover the true nature of the rune.

You may notice that your results match what you have read, or there may be some differences. If you are completely uncomfortable with your results, it is OK to repeat any of these exploration processes. Some runes are difficult to understand, others are easy. You may want to find other people who have experience with the runes and discuss your findings with them. You may be surprised by the results of this effort.

You can log your observations on the next few pages. Remember to make your observations in two steps. Start with your subconscious observations, then add your conscious. Subconscious observations should include no interpretative information, only basic sensory observations, such as colors, smells, textures, sights, sounds, visual imagery, and emotions. For your conscious observations, ask yourself what all of the subconscious, sensory information means to you. How does this rune apply to your life? Where does it fit in? Finally, write down any general thoughts that come up.

There are no wrong answers, because what you write will be your own explanation of the runes.

RUNIC MEDITATION LOG

FEHU, ᚠ: cattle, fee, money

Subconscious observations: _____

_____

Conscious observations: _____

_____

URUZ, ᚢ: aurochs, bison, strength, vitality, primal essence

Subconscious observations: _____

_____

Conscious observations: _____

_____

THURISAZ, ᚦ: thorn, giant, demon, violence

Subconscious observations: _____

_____

Conscious observations: _____

_____

ANSUZ, ᚨ: deity, consciousness, words and speaking

Subconscious observations: _____

_____

Conscious observations: _____

_____

RAIDO, R: wheel, travel

Subconscious observations: _____

_____

Conscious observations: _____

_____

KENNAZ, ⟨ : knowing, fires of the forge, creativity

Subconscious observations: _____

_____

Conscious observations: _____

_____

GEBO, ✕ : gift, generosity, giving

Subconscious observations: _____

_____

Conscious observations: _____

_____

WUNJO, Ᵽ: joy, happiness

Subconscious observations: _____

_____

Conscious observations: _____

_____

HAGALAZ, ᚺ: hail, storms, natural disruptive forces

Subconscious observations: _____

_____

Conscious observations: _____

_____

NAUTHIZ, ᚾ: need, necessity, restraints

Subconscious observations: _____

_____

Conscious observations: _____

_____

ISA, ᛁ: ice, stasis, stagnation, frozen

Subconscious observations: _____

_____

Conscious observations: _____

_____

JERA, ᛃ: year, harvest, boon, success

Subconscious observations: _____

_____

Conscious observations: _____

_____

EIHWAZ, ↲: yew tree, universal connection, world tree

Subconscious observations: _____

_____

Conscious observations: _____

_____

PERTHRO, ᚲ: fate, karma, luck

Subconscious observations: _____

_____

Conscious observations: _____

_____

ELHAZ, ᛉ: elk, protection, divine forces

Subconscious observations: _____

_____

Conscious observations: _____

_____

SOWILO, ᛋ: sun, striking force, nurtured life

Subconscious observations: _____

_____

Conscious observations: _____

_____

TIWAZ, ⇑: Tyr, focus, discipline, warrior

Subconscious observations: _____

_____

Conscious observations: _____

_____

BERKANA, ß: birch tree, fertile land, female energy

Subconscious observations: _____

_____

Conscious observations: _____

_____

EHWAZ, M: horse, movement, societal status

Subconscious observations: _____

_____

Conscious observations: _____

_____

MANNAZ, M: man, self, people

Subconscious observations: _____

_____

Conscious observations: _____

_____

LAGUZ, ↑: lake, water, depths

Subconscious observations: _____

_____

Conscious observations: _____

_____

INGUZ, ◇: Freyr, seed, male fertility

Subconscious observations: _____

_____

Conscious observations: _____

_____

DAGAZ, ⋈: day, change, 180-degree turn

Subconscious observations: _____

_____

Conscious observations: _____

_____

OTHALA, ⋈: inheritance, legacy, ancestors

Subconscious observations: _____

_____

Conscious observations: _____

_____

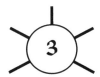

THE OUTER RUNES

Runes are singular energies that permeate throughout all things. This means that the same runic energy that came into play at the beginning of all things in this universe still exists. We can find this energy within anything and everything that exists about us. The ancients had this deeper understanding of the runes. They did not believe that the runes existed only in special places or specific times. Rather, they said the runes exist eternally within the whole world about us.

We do not have to dig too deep into the lore to find this belief. The Sigrdrifumal, a poem that is part of the Volsung saga, gives an example. This particular story is of the resurrection of Sigrdrifa, a Valkyrie or collector of the battle slain. Many will know this poem in the form of the *Niebelunglied*, or Richard Wagner's Ring Cycle. In these tales, Sigrdrifa is known as Brynhild, or Brünnhilde.

In the Volsung saga, there was a battle between two kings, Agnar and Hjalmgunnar. Odin had promised the victory to Hjalmgunnar, an aging warrior, and told Sigrdrifa to grant victory to his chosen. But Sigrdrifa refused and killed Hjalmgunnar in battle. As punishment, Odin struck Sigrdrifa with a sleep thorn, wrapped her in magical chain mail, and placed her resting form within a wall of fire. When the hero Sigurd heard what happened, he decided to win the love of this fair-famed Valkyrie. With his horse, Grani, he penetrated the wall of fire and cut the chain mail from her chest. When she awoke, Sigrdrifa spoke a sacred prayer:

Hail day, hail sons of day
Hail night and her daughter
With kind eyes, look upon us both
And grant those sitting here, victory

Hail Aesir, Hail Goddesses
Hail, to the bountiful earth.
Speech and wisdom give us noble twain,
And healing hands while we live.

As reward for awakening her, Sigrdrifa taught Sigurd the ways of the runes. This teaching involved teaching him many of the rune charms, such as the charms of birth runes, healing runes, dark runes, and many more. Included also was an initiation ceremony. In this rite, runes were carved onto wood and then scraped into a horn of mead. When this mead was consumed, the mysteries of the runes became ingrained within Sigurd. Following this ceremony, Sigurd was taught where he might find the runes:

There they are, carved on a shield,
Which stands before the shining god,
On Arvak's ear and,
On Alsvidh's hoof,
On the wheel which rolls,
Under Rognir's ear,
On Sleipnir's teeth and,
On the sledge's bands.

On the bear's paw,
And on Bragi's tongue,
On the wolfs' claws,
And on the eagles' beak,
On the bloody wings,
And on the bridges' end,
On the releasing hand,
And on the healing's track.

On glass and on gold,
And on amulets of men,
In wine and in wort,
And in the welcome seat,
On Gungnir's point,
And on Grani's breast,
On the Norn's nail,
And the owls' neb.

From these passages, one might deduce that runes are within all things everywhere. If they can be found in this list of items, it stands to reason that the runes can be found within anything. In addition, we will find that there is not just one rune by itself within an object. We will find that all objects contain all twenty-four runes within them at all times.

To the ancient people who wrote this poem, it described things that were important to them. These objects had a daily and mythological importance. The objects listed in the first stanza are all mythological in origin; the horses Arvak and Alsvidh, for example, pulled the chariots of the sun and moon across the sky each day. The second stanza is about runes occurring in natural/out-of-doors objects. The final stanza deals with home, finery, and human-oriented objects. These three stanzas place the runes in three categories: spiritual, natural, and manmade.

These three categories are still important to the people of today. We each need a spiritual connection to something. As we still need to breathe clean air, drink clean water, and eat, we are still as much a part of nature as we ever were. As humans, the embodiment of Mannaz, we make things, establish our homes in the cities, and separate ourselves from the natural world. Even though a thousand years has passed since the creation of this poem, its essential elements are the same. One could easily replace many of the objects with modern-day items, and the poem would retain its complete meaning. The only thing that would change is the relevance of the words to the average person in today's society. However, most will never encounter this poem, let alone understand its importance.

Universal Reflections

We have already explored the universal principle of similarities, which says that similarities attract and perpetuate. This principle establishes that similar minds, concepts, and objects will migrate toward each other, and sometimes they will combine to form a more complex structure. Another principle we will explore is the reflective principle. Simply stated, this principle says that the universe is a reflection of itself, in all ways.

These principles are not limited to the Norse tradition. Many other belief systems of the world use different words to state the same things. In the hermetic tradition, we find the maxim, "As above, so below. As within, so without." The intersection of the two triangles that make up the Star of David is often interpreted as a reflection of the divine in the natural world. Even in the Christian tradition is the phrase "on earth as it is in heaven." We can see that the reflective principle has been around for a very long time. Where does one need to look in the natural world to find it?

Look no further than a diagram of the solar system and compare that with a diagram of a molecule. They both have a central body encircled by smaller bodies. For the solar system, the central body is the sun; for the molecule, it is the nucleus. The orbiting bodies are planets and electrons, respectively.

Here we have the beginning of the definition of the macrocosmos and microcosmos—that is, the greater universe and the lesser universe—and the idea that one reflects the other. We can even look to the lesser universes to better explain the greater. This is exactly what quantum theorists are doing on a daily basis. As they understand the energies that make up the particles, they come to understand what makes up the whole of the universe. They even have a name for the very first energy/particle that came into existence after the big bang: the god particle.

We see this concept analogous to the hologram. Every part of a hologram contains the complete information of the whole image. If you were to cut a part of it off, you would still have all of the information of the complete picture. William Blake captured the principle in the first line of his poem "Auguries of Innocence": "To see the world in a grain of sand."

The Runic Connection

This reflective principle applies at the runic level because we can trace every object back to some form of cosmic creation. Looking at the formation of stars, solar systems, and planets, we find everything is made up of the same stuff. We can all trace the origin of everything we are and everything around us to some form of big bang. This principle establishes a Ginnic level of origin to anything we encounter. Since the runes were formed at this level of reality, they permeate all levels of existence.

However, we may find that some of the runic energy is more prominent in some objects than in others. This difference is to be expected. A table and a baseball bat may be made of the same material; however, they have different purposes. If we were to look at their Uruz (ᚢ), we notice they have the same strength that comes from the same material (oak wood). Both the baseball bat and the table have Mannaz (ᛗ) and Thurisaz (ᚦ) energy. However, the table may have more of Mannaz (ᛗ) energy, to reflect a gathering of people. The baseball bat may have more Thurisaz (ᚦ) energy to reflect its striking of the ball.

These differences also make it easier to see some runes' energy than others, and some runes' energy is easier to explain than others. For example, we can easily see an object's Fehu—the value it has, its price or personal value. The joy an object brings is its Wunjo.

Other runic energies, such as the spiritual connection an everyday object has, are quite difficult to find. It would be hard to understand a chair's Eihwaz, its universal connection, but we know it is there. We just need to understand the deeper nature of the chair and its origin.

Another difficulty one may have with seeing the Futhark in the world is that runes may have duplicate meanings. As we already saw, Fehu could have a monetary and personal value. A dollar to a rich man has less value than a dollar to a poor man. How that dollar is used by the two different people is what establishes its variant Fehu.

Another example of a rune with multiple meanings is Uruz. We see that it has the primal and bestial energies of the bison. Contained within that primal essence is its healing power. One can imagine taking the health and vitality it takes to be a professional football player and transferring that energy into a sick person. This boost could have a healing effect.

The opposite of this concept is also true. When analyzing objects, one may find multiple runes to describe the same essence. We have seen an object's value may be described by Fehu, but what if that object is an heirloom? Then the object's value is tied to Othala as well. Both a car and an airplane are large, used for transportation and travel, and can have power and prestige attached to them. For this reason, the energy of these vehicles can be defined as both Raido and Ehwaz.

All it takes to see these energies is a bit of imagination, understanding, and maybe even some meditation time. When you understand the Futhark value of an object, you begin to understand how it is connected to all things. Then you will be able to understand how everyone is connected and that humanity is not really separate from anything. This understanding leads to the goal that many spiritual traditions hold—to show us that everyone and everything is connected as a great whole. When you see the variations of runes in all things, you will understand the underlying existence of all things and what that existence is. This insight cannot be described in words, only experienced on a deeply personal level.

The Outer Futhark in Detail

The following is a list of the runes of the Elder Futhark and how they may be found in objective reality. These explanations are general and can be applied to any object of your choosing.

FEHU, ᚠ

Keywords: price, value, medium of exchange
Examples: costs, personal value, time, energy

Put simply, the Fehu of an object is its value. This value usually is the agreed-upon trading price of the object, the cost that all people are expected to pay when they purchase it. A price may not always be placed on an object, but they still have a value. There is also the personal value one may have for objects such as heirlooms, home-made objects, or naturally existing things such as the tree in the yard or the scenic view from the window.

Also connected with Fehu is how the object fits in with the world around it. Naturally occurring objects may not have monetary value, but these objects have their places and functions in nature. Therefore, the value they have can only be understood as a part of the whole ecosystem.

Fehu is the rune of the medium of exchange. Connected to that, one must also consider what is being exchanged. In the case of actions, one can exchange energy, time, manpower, or anything else that is a nontangible but quantifiable medium.

URUZ, ᚢ

Keywords: strength, health, vitality, primal nature
Examples: energy level, physical strength, resilience, untamability

Uruz can be thought of as the strength, resilience, or vitality of an object. The Uruz is much easier to find in living things than it is in non-living objects. Living creatures, such as animals, can be untamable and primal in nature, and that nature is their Uruz. We can also see that the strength of an animal such as an elephant is quite daunting.

Finding Uruz in inanimate objects might be more difficult, yet all things have strength or vitality to them. If an object has some sort of load-bearing capability, that capability is its Uruz. The Uruz of a table may be its sturdiness. Uruz is best not thought of quantitatively. Rather, the Uruz of a rock is its durability, and the Uruz of paper might be how long it lasts before fading.

THURISAZ, Þ

Keywords: destruction, aggression, anger, violence
Examples: explosiveness, temper, potential use as a weapon

The Thurisaz of an object is its destructive potential. Again, this quality is something that is easier to find in living beings. We can see the aggression of wild animals or the anger of human beings. This Thurisaz energy is readily apparent in the destructive potential of weapons. Their Thurisaz is in their function or dangerous portions. Gunpowder, poison, and sharp edges or points count as parts with Thurisaz energy.

Ordinary objects also hold this potential, though they may not seem to at first. The best way to look for the Thurisaz of an object is to realize the aggressive way the object must be used to realize its destructive potential. A log is just a just a log until wielded with aggression. Then it becomes a club.

ANSUZ, ᚨ

Keywords: thoughts, mind, understanding, awareness, communication
Examples: self-awareness, information systems, communication systems (such as the mouth or television)

Ansuz works with all things concerning information and communication. Ansuz is the information itself, as well as the storage, retrieval, and transfer of that information. This information can even be the medium of exchange found within Fehu.

In today's world, we encounter more and more objects that are designed to store and transmit information. They are the basis of the information age. We are creatures bent on keeping and passing information. Simply by being humans in the modern era, we are the caretakers of a greater understanding of Ansuz than has ever existed.

This Ansuz is found in human beings at the thought and memory level. Your ability to store and transmit information is your Ansuz. How you do it is your own unique Ansuz. There are several objects that have readily apparent Ansuzes, such as computers, radios, and televisions. It is difficult to find the Ansuz of a table, but with a bit of patience, one will see it has measurements, plus the DNA and rings of the tree its wood came from—all of which is stored information.

RAIDO, R

Keywords: travel, movement, mobility
Examples: the ability of an object to move, movement within an object

Raido is easy to find in things that move. When we speak of a vehicle, we easily see the Raido. It is the vehicle's ability to move and be driven. We see this same movement potential in living creatures. We humans walk about, snails slide along a trail of mucus, and birds fly. All forms of movement are viable definitions of Raido.

What about inanimate objects? The very word *inanimate* seems to be the opposite of what Raido means. To understand Raido in these things, we need to dig a bit deeper. Plants move water internally from the soil to the leaves. This process is their Raido. For lifeless inanimate objects, we need to stretch the imagination a bit more and resort to modern science, which tells us that every molecule of the objects is constantly moving and vibrating. This form of Raido exists at the quantum level within everything.

KENNAZ, ᚲ

Keywords: creative fire, creativity, craftsmanship, work, toil
Examples: smithing, work put into an object to make it

Kennaz represents creative processes and the potential of objects to change from one form into another. This process is the one that smiths of all types have undertaken for centuries. Kennaz is that creative spark that is put into motion. First, there needs to be an idea, and when that idea is put into motion, you have the workings of Kennaz.

The Kennaz of an inanimate object lies not in what it does, but what is done with it. It must have been crafted by a human or natural force. This action that made the object is still reflected in its nature. Therefore, we can appreciate the creative effort an artist put in the sculpture we are observing. This creative force is the sculpture's residual Kennaz.

GEBO, ✕

Keywords: gift, generosity, giving
Examples: gift exchange, fruits of a tree

To the ancients, generosity and hospitality were not only key attributes, but also requirements for a person to be honorable. Even Odin came in the guise of a poor man to test his devotees' generosity. This element we find in all manner of persons and creatures. This gift-giving potential is essential for all life to occur.

The generosity of naturally existing objects maybe not be as obvious as that of people. Plants' giving nature is seen in the oxygen and food they produce. Animals give their meat, their milk, or their hides to humans. (However, it may be argued that humans take these things from the animals, instead of the animals giving them.)

The Gebo of an inanimate object may need to be a projection of its user. A CD gives music, entertainment, and relaxation to the listener. A computer may give information. A pen gives ink that is used for writing. A business card is given to one person by another; the giving of the card, or the giving of any thing, is a complete embodiment of Gebo.

WUNJO, ᛈ

Keywords: joy, happiness
Examples: the joy one receives from using the object, the ability to feel happy

The emotional joy felt by humans and animals is Wunjo. Even plants exhibit a type of joy; increased growth and production is their exuberant response to ideal conditions.

One may think that this rune energy, being an emotion, is relegated to living things only. But inanimate objects also have Wunjo in that they have the potential to give joy. That potential must be awakened through some action. Their Wunjo is tied in with Gebo, the energy of giving and gifts. This potential to induce happiness is latent within a gifted item. While the person giving the gift feels the joy of giving it, the recipient is also filled with the joy of getting it. Yet none of this happiness would be possible without the gift itself.

HAGALAZ, ᚺ

Keywords: hail, storms, natural disaster, fury
Examples: inner turmoil, falling branches, potential for disaster

Hagalaz is the pure, naturally existing, destructive force contained within all things. In many cases, it is similar to the Thurisaz of an object. The two may not be very easy to distinguish. The Hagalaz and Thurisaz of an inanimate object may be the same exact trait.

People all have their little internal storms. These storms may be emotional, mental, or even physical. These are the disruptions that occur from time to time. These disruptions also exist within naturally occurring objects, such as in the form of a parasite or fungus. Maybe the object itself even has a naturally occurring destructive nature. Consider the falling branches of a tree. While not intentionally destructive, they can be seen that way by an unsuspecting person whose body, home, or vehicle is damaged by them.

The effects of Hagalaz may be very subtle. Inanimate objects, if not maintained and kept safe, will break down and be destroyed. Time itself may be a form of Hagalaz for all things, because all things are destroyed, little by little, over time.

NAUTHIZ, ᚾ

Keywords: need, necessity, constraint
Examples: food, water, air

The essence of Nauthiz is found in the needs of an object if it is to continue to exist. These needs are beyond the realm of wants and desires. They are what must be done or received to keep the object in its present form.

All things that exist have needs. For living creatures, they are food, air, water. For humans, they continue along the lines of Maslow's hierarchy of needs to include shelter, social status, and spiritual connection.

Inanimate objects also have their needs. Walls need to be painted and wood needs to be varnished. Otherwise the weather would destroy such objects. Electronic items need the flow of electricity to work. Works of art need shelter and protection, lest they be destroyed by the ravages of time.

ISA, ᛁ

Keywords: ice, stasis, frozen
Examples: objects that never move, parts that stay still

Up until this point in the Elder Futhark, it has been a challenge to discover the energy of the runes in inanimate objects. Sometimes we had to stretch the imagination. But Isa is ideal for inanimate objects. The word *inanimate* means these objects do not move, and lack of movement is what Isa is all about.

Sometimes the Isa of an object can be tied to its Uruz. For example, a wall is strong and stout because it does not move. The same is true for stones, furniture, or any other inanimate object.

What about animate objects? Were does Isa come into play here? Surely there are parts, internally and externally, that do not move. These parts may be the bones of mammals, shells of crustaceans, or the DNA of any living thing. With a bit of digging and some imagination, we can find the Isa within all things, animate or not.

JERA, ⟨

Keywords: year, harvest, boon, growth
Examples: success, gaining a goal, accomplishment

From the stasis of Isa and the toil of Nauthiz we are brought to the accomplishment of Jera. Within all things lies a sense of purpose and achievement. We humans set goals all the time and reach them. Our accomplishments may be as simple as getting a cup of coffee or as momentous as the achievement of weight loss.

For the animal and plant kingdoms, goals are no different. In their daily struggle to stay alive, plants and animals, too, have amassed a collection of goals. For plants, the goal is the reception of sunlight and the internal movement of water. For animals, it is consuming food, averting predators, and reproducing.

The Jera of inanimate objects consists of qualities that can potentially be brought out from within them. For a smith, the beauty of a necklace is its inherent Jera, as a more beautiful piece will fetch a higher price. The quality of craftsmanship may also be the goal. Inanimate objects, again, may need intervention for their Jera to be fully realized.

EIHWAZ, ↑

Keywords: yew tree, spiritual connection, shamanic travel
Examples: hierarchy, connection with the world, spiritual connection

Eihwaz, by its nature, is one of the most difficult runes to describe and understand. The ancients believed that humans descended from the gods. Our unique way of being open to the divine and the spiritual is our Eihwaz.

This spiritual or divine connection is not so easily seen in animals or inanimate objects, yet that connection is there. All things that exist came from some source and have some purpose. All these things will one day be destroyed and may be rebuilt into something else. Plants may become food for an animal, for example. Inanimate objects may have to go through a similar process, such as the recycling of plastic bottles into clothes, hammocks, or carpets.

Often the Eihwaz of an object is difficult to describe in words. It will often take you time in meditation to discover how an object connects to all other things. But once you discern this connection to other things, you will know the object's Eihwaz.

PERTHRO, ᚲ

Keywords: the unknowable, fate, openness
Examples: one's destiny, that which cannot be known about someone or something

The ancient Nordic people were fatalists. They believed that since everything had a beginning and an ending, everything that happened was predestined. As humans, we are to follow our destiny from point to point. Yet we are the ones who make the decisions on how we reach that destiny. Whatever choices we make, we will always live out our destinies.

Destiny, or Perthro, can be an unknowable force. We may not know our Perthro, but it is always there. Perthro may also be used to describe the fate of an object. Ask what is the purpose of this object, where is it going, or what will be done with it? With the answers to those questions, the object's Perthro may be discovered.

ELHAZ, ᛉ

Keywords: elk, protection, higher spiritual forces
Examples: barbed wire, white light, varnish

In the environment we live in, there is something out to destroy everything. Outside destructive force can be perceived as the Thurisaz and the Hagalaz of the object. To continue to exist, this object needs some sort of protection to counteract external Thurisaz and Hagalaz energies.

For all living things, there is a line of defense. Externally, it includes skin, fur, teeth, nails, claws, and sometimes appearance. For internal protection, there is the immune system. This immune system, because it uses an active, destructive process, has a connection with a protective aspect of Thurisaz.

Our spiritual side also needs protection. We find it in a connection with the higher spiritual forces. Some people choose to see this protection as white light, others as the hammer of Thor. We do know there is a form of protective energy, and we all have different ways to see it.

Inanimate objects, too, need a layer of protection. It could take the form of paint or varnish. A home left to the freezing and thawing temperatures would be destroyed by the changes, but maintaining a constant temperature in a home is an act of protection.

SOWILO, ᛋ

Keywords: sun, power, energy
Examples: internal energy, a power source, explosive potential

The ancients saw the sun as having two aspects. They saw that it could destroy icebergs and that objects left out in it would fade and decompose. They also saw its nurturing force, giving plants their life. The Sowilo found in objects also has these two aspects.

With living creatures, the source of the power is at the cellular level, where food is turned into energy. With people, this power could metaphorically describe one's motivation and drive.

With inanimate objects, finding the Sowilo can be difficult. We can ask if the object generates some sort of energy, such as heat or light. If it doesn't, there may be something happening at the molecular level. Every object has some sort of potential energy. For example, a table can be burned or dropped, thereby releasing thermal or gravitational energy.

TIWAZ, ᛏ

Keywords: Tyr, discipline, focus, duty, responsibility
Examples: routine, singular functions, structure

Everything adheres to some sort of structure. This structure can be found right within the genetic code of all living things. All things grow according to this inherent plan.

We find the Tiwaz of nonliving things within their function and structure. Be they computer or table, these objects were designed with a plan in mind, and they may serve a singular function. This function is the essence of Tiwaz.

The same sense of structure, of Tiwaz, is represented by a sense of duty, responsibility and routine with people. This Tiwaz energy is what enabled Tyr to sacrifice his hand to stop the wolf. He knew what needed to be done to stop the destruction by the wolf. We see this same sense of order when we rise each morning to go to work. We know the structure and discipline we need to follow in order to continue to survive.

BERKANA, ᛒ

Keywords: birch tree, nurturing, fertility
Examples: womb, fertile land, any potential source of growth

Berkana represented, to the ancient Nordic peoples, the fertility of the field and of female creatures. This fertility was often represented by goddesses. Goddesses were also the disseminators of hospitality. So any person who has a nurturing and giving side has an active Berkana within them.

This same functionality must exist within all living things for them to thrive. No living thing survives on its own. It must derive nutrition from some source. That source may be the living thing's mother or the nutrients that the thing feeds from.

However it exists, there is some form of growth potential that all things have within them. A pen may have a pregnant belly of ink ready to burst. A glass holds water in it. Both of these things are examples of the Berkana that exists within inanimate objects.

EHWAZ, ᛗ

Keywords: horse, movement, stature
Examples: rank or title, swift and powerful movement, status symbology

Princes of the old ages were renowned for their power and prestige. This tradition follows through to us in the modern day; only instead of royalty, social status is the key to renown. Most people living in first-world countries live like the kings of a thousand years ago. Modern vehicles, homes, and clothing tend to have a readily apparent Ehwaz built right in.

For naturally existing things, Ehwaz is in the hierarchical nature of existence. In herds and packs, the leader of the pack shows his Ehwaz when he struts about the others. For trees, look no further than their height and stoutness to identify their status.

Everyday objects do have a taste of Ehwaz within them as well. Often, the Fehu of an object is a direct reflection of its Ehwaz. One can buy a one-dollar pen at the grocery store or a fifty-dollar pen from a specialty store. The Ehwaz of the fifty-dollar pen gives it a higher stature than the one-dollar pen.

MANNAZ, ᛗ

Keywords: man, mankind, the self
Examples: names, species, identification

Mannaz is the essence of what separates mankind from the rest of the animals: intelligence, the ability to use tools, the basic, natural inability to defend one's self in a natural setting. For this reason, mankind separated itself from the natural world. This separation dictated the need to distinguish a rune unique to mankind. In the animal kingdom, Mannaz is first found in the name of the animal. Secondarily, an animal's Mannaz would be a common trait shared by its entire species, such as the stripes of a tiger, the size of a hippopotamus, or the teeth of a shark.

When it comes to objects, the Mannaz of that object can first be its name. Where Tiwaz could be the function and purpose of the object, Mannaz would be the brand name of the product. Also, just as we have a connection to the rest of humanity, the object may have a connection to all the other objects similar to it. Even though there are different brands of vacuum cleaners, a vacuum cleaner is still a vacuum cleaner, like all the others. The Mannaz of an object is what it shares in common with other objects of the same type, as well as what makes it unique to other types of objects.

LAGUZ, ᛚ

Keywords: lake, water, mysteries, flow
Examples: subconscious, emotions, psychic ability

There is an obvious connection between water and all living things on planet Earth. They all need water to live. The human body is over 80 percent water. In a literal sense, water is the Laguz of the human body. Indeed, it is the Laguz of all living things.

Beyond that Laguz has other subtle meanings. It is the part of the psyche that feels and dreams. This ability to feel emotions and have dreams is something that we share with most other animals, as science is starting to discover.

The flow of rivers, streams, and waterfalls is something that Laguz covers. We see this flow in plants as they move water around within themselves and in animals as they move blood and fluids around within their bodies. This same thing exists in electronic devices. As electric current is introduced, the electrons flow from one molecule into another. This flow is Laguz's character.

INGUZ, ◇

Keywords: Freyr, seed, male fertility, potential energy
Examples: seeds, ideas, concepts

Buried within all things is the potential of what they may become. As we have seen, all things can be destroyed and then rebuilt into something else. This potential that exists within the physical nature of all things is what Inguz represents.

To humanity, Inguz could be the start of something new. It is the idea or concept of a plan to be put into motion. For this plan to be a success, it needs to be enacted in a fertile environment. This potential for growth is what Inguz is all about. The question in play is, what can this become?

On a physical level, the nature of Inguz is apparent in the male sperm that must find its way to the female egg for new life to begin.

The Inguz of everyday things is what they contain. Water within a glass is the glass's Berkana. Its Inguz is the exact same thing, only it takes a person tilting the glass or putting a straw into it for the glass's full potential to be achieved. For the pen that contains ink, the act of writing is its Inguz.

DAGAZ, ᛞ

Keywords: day, change, transformation
Examples: death, change of form, evaporation, usage

We are dying from the moment we are born. Our cells grow and die all the time. We are constantly renewing all parts of our body and soul. This transformative process is at the heart of Dagaz.

When looking at various objects, one must ask, what is changing about them? What part of them changes and how? For instance the finish of a table may darken with age. Even inanimate objects have some sort of transformative power. Like other runes, this potential may be latent, and it takes the actions of a person or other such creature for that transformation to be realized. For example, when you put a table into a room, that room is transformed into a dining room.

OTHALA, ᛟ

Keywords: inheritance, legacy, home
Examples: house, property, heirlooms, genetics

All things that exist have one thing in common: they must have come from something. The origination object and the new object both retain the same characteristics in some way. This connection to its origin is the object's Othala. For example, if a wall is made of wood, then it owes its nature to the type of tree it came from.

Living things bear the genetic code of their parents and ancestors. Genetic scientists are now showing that there is recumbent DNA—that is, little strands of genetic information that are turned off—

in all living things. If this information were turned on, a person could grow a tail or gills. This fact shows us that we still bear a connection to all manner of living things, and this connection is another example of Othala.

When it comes to house and hearth, there is no better rune than Othala. For the past ages, Othala directly referred to the land and house that a person was living in. The Othala of a turtle or snail is instantly identified as its shell as well as its genetic code.

Exercise 3: The Futhark in All Things

We have seen how the runes of the Elder Futhark can be uncovered in all things. Now the task at hand is to take ordinary objects, one by one, and give a runic definition to them. You will be able to find the energy of each of the twenty-four runes in any object you choose. Doing so may take time, meditation, study, and reflection, but it will give you a deeper understanding of the natures of all the runes. You will also gain a deeper connection with your self and all things around you.

This exercise is your opportunity to take what you have learned of the runes from previous exercises and see it in the world around you. Simply take each of the objects identified and contemplate the existence of that object from the perspective of the Elder Futhark. The runic energies of the first object, a boat, are listed as an example. Following that are objects found in everyday life: an airplane and a tree. For the final part of the exercise, you are to pick your own object to describe using the Futhark.

You will soon see that every single rune of the Futhark exists in all things. Some runes may be more prevalent in certain objects and less obvious in others. In fact, some of the runes may perfectly describe the object. Conversely, you may need to stretch your imagination and understanding of a rune to see how it is applicable to the object.

Let's take an ice cube for example. The rune Isa (l) best fits the ice cube. It will be a stretch to find how Sowilo (ϟ) fits in. Perhaps if you look to the molecular level you may see it. All the molecules still have an energy and movement—Thurisaz (Þ) and Raido (ᚱ) about them. In some way, every rune exists in all things.

The questions on the following pages will help you think about the nature of the runes within objects—the outer runes. Many runic characteristics will be similar from object to object; other characteristics may differ greatly. The Futhark energies of a boat have been listed first as an example. The Futhark energies found in an airplane, which you are asked to list, may be similar to those of a boat. Both airplanes and boats transport people in very different ways. The Futhark of the tree may prove to be a challenge. A tree is living, yet not mobile, plus there is a great deal of mythology that surrounds different types of trees. If you were to compare the Futhark energies of two different trees, you might find many of the runic energies of a pine tree are the same as those of an oak tree. There also may be stark contrasts.

After you have practiced finding the energies of an airplane and a tree, choose an object of your own and describe its Futhark.

All of the answers come from your understanding of the runes and your perception of the world around you.

The Futhark of a Boat

ᚠ   The money paid for the boat and the value the boat has to the people who use it. If it is a working boat, it provides income for the crew.

ᚢ   This is the engine or motor the boat has; the bigger the boat, the stronger the engine.

ᚦ   The boat is designed to slice through the waves and the water. The propeller churns up water. The military also uses boats and ships for warfare.

ᚨ   Some boats have computers and navigation systems. A person needs to be trained and skilled in sailing in order to successfully pilot a boat.

ᚱ   A boat's primary function is to carry people and material over a distance on water. This ability to travel and transport is the essential nature of Raido.

ᚲ   The craftsmanship and skill used to make a boat. Kennaz also represents the labor that a working boat, such as a tugboat or freighter, does.

ᚷ   The gift the boat gives people is the ability to travel over water at great speeds and protection from the water. The boat itself may even be given as a gift.

ᚹ   For many, boating is a pleasurable experience. What is it about traveling in the boat that makes it a joy for the boater? This answer is, of course, subjective and will vary from person to person.

ᚺ   There are many hazards one encounters with a boat. Collisions do happen. One may encounter storms or any manner of mechanical problems with a boat. A boat may collect barnacles and be subjected to the ravages of rust.

ᚾ   Any boat needs regular maintenance, from mechanical repairs to painting and general sprucing up. Its engine may need gasoline for power and oil for lubrication.

ᛁ   A boat has a rigid and unchanging structure. It is said that changing the name of a boat is unlucky.

ᚹ Great success can be had from a boat. Working boats enable successful commerce; recreational boats can enable you to successfully enjoy fishing, water sports, and other recreational activities.

ᛁ Many different cultures use boats all over the world. The same boating techniques may be used by boaters everywhere.

ᚲ It is too simple to say that the boat is there because it is meant to be there. The actions performed by and on the boat are part of the larger scheme. Does the boat bring in food for many people to eat and money for others to sustain their families with? Does the boat provide a moment of relaxation and vacation so a person can better function in his or her own busy life?

ᚤ Many a seafarer gains a deep bond with the sea. The weekend sailor also gains a deep association with water. These connections can almost be thought of as spiritual connections. We do have a great deal of lore concerning sea creatures and spirits. There are rune spells used to calm a sea or raise a fair ocean wind.

ᛋ Sowilo is the power of the boat's movement—what fuels the engine, the physical strength used to row the boat or gasoline. It is also the engine's process of internal combustion.

ᛏ Tiwaz is the discipline used to operate the boat. What maritime rules and regulations does the boat's operator or crew have to follow? If there's a crew, what is the chain of command? What unspoken rules of the water—its movement, its depth, its temperature—must be obeyed in order for the boat to stay afloat and for those aboard to use the boat safely and successfully?

ᛒ Berkana is the good that comes from the boat's use. This is its latent potential. Can it be used to bring in a great harvest of fish, or is it used to have a great amount of fun?

ᛗ The status of a person that owns a boat is generally taken into consideration. Is it a yacht or a rowboat? What is the cost of the boat? Is it a luxury item or a useful tool?

ᛗ This is the type of boat. Does it have a brand name or designation? What is the boat's name and identity? Every boat has a unique personality. Mannaz is the indicator of that personality.

ᛚ What parts of the boat flow? Does it have fuel and engine fluid lines? Certainly the water flows around the hull of the boat.

ᚶ What does the boat initiate? The spark from its engine's spark plugs is one form of initiation. The boat could spark ideas of trips to take and financial goals that can be accomplished with it. Since Inguz has the aspect of encasement, the lower decks fall into this category. The hull of the boat keeps the crew and machinery safe from the water.

ᛞ There is some part of the boat that is ever changing. It may constantly collect barnacles and need to be scrubbed off. It needs regular painting and finishing. The location of a boat is always changing.

ᛟ Many boats are part of a long line of improvements. The Othala of a boat simply could mean its make and model. Maybe its design can be traced back to the schooner days or to Native American canoes.

The Futhark of an Airplane

ᚠ The trade value or worth of the object. Is it a monetary value or personal value?

_____

ᚢ The power and strength of the airplane. Does it exert force or have some sort of structural strength?

_____

ᚦ The plane's aggressive or directed energy. In what way can it be used aggressively?

_____

ᚨ The communication or understanding level of the plane. Does it have a programmed function? Or what knowledge is required to use it?

_____

ᚱ   The mobility inside or outside of the airplane. Does it move? What sort of movement takes place in or around it?

_____

ᚲ   The airplane's creative force. Is it used for or does it inspire creative energy? Was it made?

_____

ᚷ   The giving aspect of the plane. Does it do something for others or can it be given as a gift?

_____

ᚹ   The joy that comes from the plane's existence. Is there some manner in which an airplane creates happiness or alleviates suffering?

_____

ᚻ   The commotion caused by the plane. What is the stormy nature connected to it?

_____

ᚾ   The airplane's need or needs. What fuel or maintenance does it need to function correctly? Does it create need or restrictions?

_____

ᛁ   The plane's stability and rigidity. What aspects or parts of the airplane never move or change?

_____

ᛃ   The success of the plane. What does it accomplish and how does it do it? Is acquiring or successfully flying the plane someone's goal?

_____

ᛇ   The universal nature of the plane. Can other cultures understand its use and function? What objects are similar to the airplane or can be used in a similar way?

_____

ᚲ How the airplane fits into the bigger picture. Is it part of a larger system? How does it fit into that system?

_____

ᛦ The spirituality and protective nature of the plane. What spiritual or protective nature does it have?

_____

ᛋ The plane's directed energy. What kind of energy does it consume or give off?

_____

ᛏ The discipline of the plane or the discipline needed to operate it. What sort of direct, focused function does it have or require?

_____

ᛒ The plane's fertility. How does it reproduce or produce anything with its function? What same actions does it repeat?

_____

ᛗ The plane's social status or the status that it confers. Where does it rank or how does it compare with other things in the various categories it belongs to—such as other airplanes, other flying objects, other forms of transportation, or other things in a person's possession?

_____

ᛗ The plane's identity. What brand is it? Does it have a name? Does it belong to, and thus carry the name of, a particular company? What type of plane is it (passenger jet, cargo plane, F16 combat jet, a crop duster)?

_____

ᚱ The flow or mystery of the plane. What part of this plane flows, or what flows around it? Is the plane easy to understand, or is there something about it that needs to be unraveled?

_____

◇ The plane's spark of initiation. What parts of the plane work on their own or within a contained system (like a seed about to sprout)?

_____

ᛉ The ever-changing part of the plane. What part of an airplane changes and continues to change? Does it ever change anything around it?

_____

ᛊ The plane's inherent and stable value. If it is passed on to someone, what sort of value or equity does it have?

_____

The Futhark of a Tree

ᚠ Subjective or objective value:

ᚢ Strength, structural or otherwise:

ᚦ Directed energy or aggression:

ᚨ Knowledge or wisdom of the tree, or knowledge or wisdom needed to use it:

_____

ᚱ Movement, internal or external:

ᚲ Work or creative potential: _____

ᚷ Giving or gift nature: _____

ᚹ Joy it gives or is found with its use: _____

ᚺ Hazards or commotions: _____

ᚾ Needs of or created by it: _____

ᛁ Stability or rigidity of it: _____

ᛃ Successfulness of it: _____

ᛏ Its universal nature: _____

ᚴ How it fits into the bigger picture: _____

ᛉ Protective nature or part: _____

ᛋ Power or fuel: _____

ᛏ Discipline or focus of it or someone who uses it: _____

ᛒ Goods or fertility: _____

ᛗ Social status of the tree or its owner: _____

ᛘ Identity; name, description, classification: _____

ᛚ Parts that flow: _____

◇ Seedling nature, containment, spark of initiation: _____

ᛦ Changing, evolving nature or parts: _____

ᚷ Legacy or inherent nature: _____

The Futhark of _____

ᚠ Subjective or objective value: _____

ᚢ Strength, structural or otherwise: _____

ᚦ Directed energy or aggression: _____

ᚨ Knowledge or wisdom within the object or that is to needed to use it:

_____

ᚱ Movement, internal or external: _____

ᚲ Work or creative potential: _____

ᚷ Giving or gift nature: _____

ᚹ Joy that it gives or that is found with its use: _____

ᚺ Hazards or commotions: _____

ᚼ   Needs of or created by the object: _____

ᛁ   Stability or rigidity of it: _____

ᛉ   Successfulness of it: _____

ᛁ   Its universal nature: _____

ᚴ   How it fits into the bigger picture: _____

ᛘ   Protective nature or part: _____

ᛋ   Power or fuel: _____

ᛏ   Discipline or focus of object or its user: _____

ᛒ   Goods or fertility: _____

ᛗ   Social status of the object or owner: _____

ᛙ   Identity; name, description, classification: _____

ᚱ   Parts that flow: _____

◇   Seedling nature, containment, spark of initiation: _____

ᛥ   Changing, evolving nature or parts: _____

ᛪ   Legacy or inherent nature: _____

THE INNER RUNES

By now, you have come to understand how the runes of the Elder Futhark exist within all things. The energy of the runes also exists within individual people at the inner level.

One can take the runes of the Elder Futhark and use them to describe the traits of any human being. Yet this objective description would not be able to describe the subjective aspects of an individual's inner world; that is to say, we could use the same runes, in the same ways, to describe different people at the You level. In fact, the answers may be very similar. But when it comes to the you level of runic description, there is a vast deviation in answers from person to person.

Connecting Spiritually with the Runes

As you learn to apply each of the runes to yourself, you will begin to understand deeper aspects of your inner being. You will see how well you perform in situations involving communication, creativity, or business sense, or in any other type of situation.

The runes, being part of an ancient spiritual tradition, are spiritual in nature. As you begin to understand your runic connection to the world, you will also gain a deeper understanding of your spiritual self, how you fit in with all levels of reality, and just how strong your connection to everything really is.

There are two runes that are best used to understand this process: Perthro (K) and Eihwaz (J). If you use these runes to analyze the character of an individual, it may be difficult to apply words to describe this person. Therefore, the process is best used to analyze only your you level of reality. After all, there is only one person who knows you best. That person is you.

Perthro is best utilized to understand your connection with your fate. This rune will show you how you fit into all levels of the world about you. Your connection with Perthro is also seen with luck. You can analyze exactly how things go in your life. Are you frustrated a lot, or do things come easily? The Norse believed in a part of the soul complex called the *Hamingja*. This part is the repository of luck. It can be tuned into a wide spectrum of positive and negative. If it is tuned to a more positive nature, positive situations are drawn to a person. The converse is also true. As a person engages in negative actions, negative situations are attracted. This concept is reflected in the Hindu tradition of Karma.

Tied in with the concept of Karma are the lessons learned in life, which is what Perthro represents as well. As you move through the various stages in your life, you will notice patterns emerging. These patterns reveal what you need to learn and what you need to teach. It is best to avoid punitive thoughts about this matter. Punishment is not a part of the energy of Perthro. Rather it is the energy of what you must experience, what you must learn, and what you need to do in order to advance.

As stated before, a good part of Norse values lies with people increasing their might and main. How those people achieve their goals is tied in with the consequences of their actions. How you live your life is how your life is. This principle also applies to the Hamingja and Perthro. Perthro describes what you do in your life, how you think about yourself, and the limitations you set determine exactly what comes to bear in your reality. If you are not pleased, do not despair. The energy can be modified and enhanced to bring about the reality you wish to have.

Eihwaz is the other rune you will need to consider when you begin to understand your spiritual nature. The energy of Eihwaz is that connection that exists throughout all the worlds. It is best represented by the great world tree, Yggdrasil. This tree is said to have connections to all the worlds of Norse cosmology. It has three great roots that stretch into the world of elves, the world of giants, and the land of the dead. Its branches also reach all the way to the highest points of Asgardh, the realm of the gods.

All over the tree are creatures that are constantly gnawing and feeding off of it. In its lowest depths is the serpent Nidhog, who grinds the bones of the dead deep within the well called Hvergelmir. From this great cauldron, all waters flow. Here we have the imagery of death and rebirth into a new form. At the highest points of the tree are harts (red deer), which feed from the leaves. From the harts' antlers drip dews that replenish life throughout the worlds. Again, we see the concept of death and renewal.

To see how you are connected with Eihwaz, you need to look at all aspects of your spiritual nature. We all have higher and lower functions, as evidenced in a Norse saying: "No man is so evil as to not have a bit of good; no man is so good as to not have a bit of evil." This constant dichotomy and balance is what is most important when considering your Eihwaz. You must look at your brilliant shining aspects and take stock of your darker side as well.

Our dark side acts like a mirror. When we understand the needs, desires, and actions of the parts of us we repress and hide, we begin to understand why we do certain things. The parts of us that we keep hidden will find a voice somewhere, somehow. These parts usually exist in a place where words cannot, so it is important to feel these parts with your emotions. In fact, these parts of ourselves may be things about ourselves that we do not wish to see and understand. For that reason, we may not wish to give words to them. Yet these darker, hidden things are truly parts of everyone and must be considered when looking at the spiritual nature.

If you find that you are not happy with what you see, again, do not despair. Just like the energy of Perthro, Eihwaz is tunable. The difference is that Eihwaz is infinitely more complex. It can be broken down into many different parts. As you break it down, you can work to energize the aspects that you do like simply by giving more attention to them and accepting them. Again, you must not ignore or disassociate yourself from your darker parts, because they will always find a way to surface. Instead, you would be wise to find a way to positively accentuate them.

There is another thing to consider when doing a spiritual analysis of your "you." When examining the runes, you may find that you have a great spiritual connection with a rune that you hadn't expected to be spiritual in nature. All runes are spiritual in nature, and that nature may be more obvious with some runes than others. Some people may find a deep spiritual affinity with the rune Thurisaz, a rune typified by powerful energy that is usually used in a destructive way. Some people may not see destructive energy as negative. They may find this energy empowering and able to be used it in a positive way. Others may choose to shun the energy of Thurisaz because they see its destructive nature as purely negative.

There is absolutely nothing wrong with either opinion; both are correct. The task of understanding the runes is one that must be done at a deeply personal level. Just as we are all individuals, our explanation of the runes will also be individualistic. Where one person sees Fehu as tied in with greed and the absorption of wealth by nefarious means, another will see Fehu as having a giving and generous nature. Remember what the rune poems had to say about Fehu: "the cause of discord among men" and "wealth is a comfort to all men." This dichotomy shows exactly how two different people could interpret the same energy differently and both be correct.

A Personal Runic Analysis

When you undertake the process of a runic self-analysis, you will discover things about your self that you may have been unaware of. Our subconscious mind is the repository of all that we understand about ourselves and the world about us. Our memories, our emotions, and all other aspects of ourselves are stored as feelings, images, and impressions. The subconscious mind is another place where words do not exist, making it difficult for the subconscious and conscious minds to easily communicate.

The subconscious mind is a place of only abstractions and impressions. The processing power needed to make facts concrete and solid resides solely within the conscious mind. Runes help us to cross this barrier. All the runes have a dualistic nature. They have a solid name and solid form, which is appealing to the conscious mind. Runes also have an emotional, energetic impression that the subconscious works with. When we connect with an individual rune, we first connect with the solid, conscious aspects of it. At the same time, the subconscious is triggered. The subconscious likes to be heard and understood, and it will respond accordingly.

When you are in a meditative state and reflecting on the runes, your first connection will be to consciously apply them. At the same time, you will be filled with a feeling. They may even trigger a visible or audible memory. Maybe you will have some other form of unworded impression. These reactions are indications that there is something more to be explored on that rune.

When this impression happens, allow it to take over. Willingly explore it, but only for as long as you are comfortable with it. If you find that you are being taken to a place that arouses nervousness or anxiety, take a break. You may choose to visit the impression at a later time.

When you do this runic self-analysis process, certain truths of who the "you" aspect of yourself is will come to light. You will begin to discern strengths you never knew you had. For example, if you are exploring Uruz, you may be filled with a surge of strength in your legs. As you explore this surge, you may find that your body is telling you to walk or run. At this point, it may be a good idea to indulge the urge. Take a walk. As you do, you may discover a new exercise program that will benefit your overall health.

Another example: if you focus on Tiwaz, you may notice that the "noise" in your mind quiets or disappears. You will know that at any future time, focusing on the energy of Tiwaz will help you think clearly and focus on the task at hand. This reaction is an indication that your Tiwaz, your mental focus and clarity, is a strength.

The converse is also true. As you focus on a particular rune, you may feel a drain or sense of emptiness. If this were to happen with the Uruz rune, try to sense where in your body you feel the drain. This feeling could indicate that you may have a physical condition that needs to be checked out by a doctor. At the personality level, as you focus on Tiwaz, you may notice a mental block take over. This block could be an indication that you have an issue keeping you from singular thinking or focusing on one subject.

Neither of these situations are reasons to assume there is something wrong with you. Your subconscious is simply communicating with you through the medium of the runes. It is trying to tell you which energies you need to focus on in order to improve and resolve any blocks. We are all composite beings and contain all of the energies of the runes within us. All that is needed is a deeper exploration of how that rune fits in with your nature. This exploration is done with meditation, internal focus using the runes.

The Inner Runes in Detail

FEHU, ᚠ

Keywords: self-worth, personal value, self-esteem
Examples: the giving and receiving of personal insights and judgments

Fehu, as stated before, is the rune of the medium of exchange. The wealth Fehu represents can cause discord or can be a joy. Since we are now looking at the aspects of your personality, an appropriate question is, what do you have an abundance of? You may look to see if this abundance causes jealousy among others or if it is something that you give freely of.

The ancient rulers who were most revered were the ones who were generous with their wealth. Is there some part of you that you give freely? There always is. Now look at this aspect and, knowing you have it, ask if it is something that you are proud of. Is it also something others will hold you in esteem for?

Fehu is simply what part of you that you give freely. Some choose to call this concept self-esteem, self-worth, or personal value. Your impression of yourself may differ from how others see you. Remember that the energy of Fehu is always a give-and-take process. Can you also take for yourself what you give?

URUZ, ᚢ

Keywords: inner and outer strength, animalistic nature
Examples: resilience, athletic ability, instinctual behavior

The energy of Uruz is that of primal natures. The aurochs was a species of bison indigenous to Europe. It was renowned for its strength and feared for its ferocity. Its large horns were coveted. The energy of Uruz reflects the energy of this large, ferocious beast. This energy is not the part of you that thinks about what it does or takes time to reflect on repercussions. You will find this energy in your internal world, in the places where you act upon instinct, in the places where you act before you think. For some, many parts of the personality have this energy. Others may have a hard time finding it, but will if they persist.

Uruz is also a reflection of strength, vitality, health, and resilience. Simply look at your self and analyze your physical status. Are you physically strong? Do you move quickly or slowly? The energy of Uruz can be reflected in the immune system. Do you get sick easily or rarely? When you do get sick, do you recover quickly?

Looking at all of these aspects of your self, you will gain a deeper understanding of your Uruz, your primal and physical nature.

THURISAZ, ᚦ

Keywords: violence, destruction, anger
Examples: temper, need for self-defense

The energy of Thurisaz is dynamic and powerful. It always takes action. There is little to no thought in the processes governed by the energies of Thurisaz. It is the rune of the giants known as Thurses. They were the primal and destructive entities that, as lore has it, were bent on the destruction of man- and godkind. Also associated with this rune is the energy of Thor. He is the protector of man- and godkind. His energy is homogenous with that of the Thurses but focused in the direction of preservation.

When it comes to the energy of the self, you must look at this aspect of your psyche. Destruction need not be a bad thing. It is necessary in order to rebuild and renew. In the world of Midgardh, sometimes violence is required for people to protect themselves. Look no further than martial arts and self-defense classes to see Thurisaz in action.

When looking for your Thurisaz, try to find what sets you off. Is there a particular topic that makes you angry? Is this anger a form of self-protection? Does this anger rise as some unconscious reaction? Look for your triggers. They will be different for everyone. Also look at your temperament. Are you easily angered, or do you have a long fuse? All of these dynamic energetic traits are tied directly into your Thurisaz energy.

ANSUZ, ᚠ

Keywords: Odin, information, communication
Examples: the conscious mind, information processing, areas of excellence for communication skills

While the energies of Uruz and Thurisaz are tied to unthinking, primal action, Ansuz is their antithesis. The energy of Ansuz deals with action of the conscious mind. Covered here is the ability to absorb, retain, and communicate information. This is the realm of Odin. Odin is said to feast only on wine, an ancient metaphor for poetry and inspiration, which are elegant expressions of words and wisdom.

Your Ansuz is your ability to process information. Can you easily absorb and retain information? What about your recall? Can you easily pull the information from your mind? Also, how easy is it for you to communicate? Look to find if words come easily for you or if they are difficult. Note if words take different routes. Some may easily compose poetry, others prose. Others may find that they excel at communicating nonverbally, such as through mathematics, art, or music.

RAIDO, R

Keywords: movement, wheel, travel
Examples: walking, running, and other forms of movement; the desire to travel; commuting

The energy of Raido was described by the ancients as the wheel— the wheel found on wagons and carts. Connected with Raido is the sense of movement and the fact that this movement can be sacred. Often the lore points to the use of these wagons for the movement of statues of gods. Thor and Freya, the sun and moon, were carried in chariots. Burial sites show that women revered for their mystical connections were buried with wagons.

The most apparent place to find your Raido is in how you move. How often are you up and about, or are you mainly sedentary? Some may find they prefer to run or ride a bicycle. Others may have the use of wheelchairs or other devices to aid in mobility. All are valid forms of Raido.

Tied in with Raido is the sense of travel. When looking to your self, ask if you are easily overcome with wanderlust or if you prefer to stay home. The energy of Raido can also be found in the You level of existence when you look to your daily commute. Is it long or short? And how do you commute?

KENNAZ, ⟨

Keywords: the forge, creative fire, smithing
Examples: creativity, physical skills, labor

The energy of Kennaz is traditionally associated with that of the Svartalfar, or dwarves. They are the subterranean master smiths capable of crafting anything. Usually those seeking a magical tool or weapon would set a form of payment, along with raw material, before a grave mound late at night. When they returned to the mound, they would find the dwarf-made tool or weapon.

When looking for Kennaz in yourself, look at what talents you have. Do you have a hobby or any other hands-on skills? Some may find that working with arts and crafts comes easily; others may prefer larger building processes. You can also look to your level of creativity. Do ideas flow easily? How easy is it for you to implement those ideas? Implementation is where skills tie in with creativity. Fortunately, skills can be honed and enhanced to match one's creativity. Creativity can also be developed. Kennaz is always changing.

Since the energy deals with the creative fire of the smith's forge, we can also find Kennaz associated with physical labor. The efforts of construction workers, road crews, or those doing any other sort of manual job, require a developed skill. The people who hang drywall have perfected their craft so they can hang it quickly and perfectly. Kennaz is ideally suited to describe such skills and effort.

GEBO, ✕

Keywords: gifts, generosity, hospitality
Examples: generous nature, amicable bonds with other people

To the ancient Nordic peoples, generosity and hospitality were vital to survival. Rulers who were well thought of were said to be "ring breakers," "free with gold," or "haters of money." These monikers were statements of praise for generous and well-paying rulers. Even common people who were generous and hospitable were said to be favored by the gods. The lore shows Odin would disguise himself as a human in order to test his followers' generosity.

The Gebo energy of the individual is associated with his or her generous nature. Look to your self and ask how freely you give. When you have something, is it open and available for the use of your friends and family? When you have something nice, do you tend to hoard it and keep it for yourself?

With all of the giving tied with Gebo comes the bonds it creates with other people. A person of generous nature may have a great deal of friends and admirers. A person who gives too much may have people that take advantage of them. The Havamal cautions that a gift demands a gift. There is always something that comes in return for the gift. This return may be a beneficial karmic return, or it may enable a codependent lifestyle. It may take some time and honesty to determine whether the return on your gift is positive or negative.

WUNJO, ᛈ

Keywords: happiness, joy
Examples: the state of contentment, being at peace, the things that make you happy

The first aett of the Elder Futhark is rounded out by the runes of gift-giving and the joy that results from it. While not all gifts provide joy, the energy of Wunjo is the positive energy that comes from those that do. Wunjo has the ability to clear the clouds of despair, leaving one elated and at peace.

When looking to your self, the basic question is, what makes you happy? Look to all the elements that make up the you level of existence. What is it that gets deep to the core of your being and brings about joy or even full-blown jollity? Lately, there has been a lot of research and work done to help people get in touch with their inner child. This inner child is the part of one's self that remembers how to play. This part of us still has a sense of wonderment and curiosity.

The energy of Wunjo taps straight into the core of the happy inner child. When delving deep into your psyche, this part of you may be obvious. Sometimes it may take some deeper self-study. Keep in mind that the part of you that was once a joyful child still exists somewhere within you. Try to remember back to when you were a child. What was it that made you happy? Do these same things, or some evolution of them, still make you happy? These are the things in which you will find your Wunjo.

HAGALAZ, ᚺ

Keywords: hail, storms, natural disasters
Examples: self-destructiveness, inner turmoil, frustrations

The energy of Hagalaz is that of the unstoppable storm from the destructive side of nature. Thurisaz represents the hateful giants bent on destruction of mankind. By contrast, Hagalaz represents the perceived destructive nature of the Jotuns—the personifications of storms, plagues, volcanic eruptions, or any sort of natural disaster.

Internally, we have this Hagalaz energy. We have all experienced the internal storms that swell and finally subside. Hagalaz is the part of our nature that causes anxiety

We may find that we are driven to do things that are not in our best interest, such as binge eating, heavy drinking, drug use, or any manner of self-destructive actions. But these self-destructive actions are not the Hagalaz energy. Instead, your Hagalaz is that part of you that *creates* these destructive behaviors, just as the Jotuns created the storms.

Discovering your Hagalaz will take some deep analysis and self-care. You will also need to employ a healthy sense of honesty with yourself. This Hagalaz part of your nature may not be entirely self-destructive. Lodge-pole pine seeds can open only after a fire; volcanic soil is the most nutrient-rich soil. This part of you that is stirring up storms may just be a part of you looking to renew and will restore you to a healthier and stronger nature. Be open with yourself, and you may be surprised by what you find.

NAUTHIZ, ᚾ

Keywords: needs, necessities, constraints
Examples: food, air, water, connections with people, anything you need to survive

The energy of Nauthiz is that which permeates all living things at the physical level. In order for anything living to continue existing, it needs to fulfill various needs. Often, these needs take the form of food, air, and water. The physical needs required for you to survive and thrive are going to be fairly obvious.

What about the needs of one's emotional, mental, and spiritual well-being? These needs will be as diverse as all of humanity. We all have different things that bring us joy, peace, and a sense of satisfied contentment. In fact, peace, joy, and contentment may well be needs. Someone who is in constant distress cannot thrive. He or she may be just barely surviving.

Take stock of your self. What is it that you deeply and truly need to be alive mentally, emotionally, and spiritually? For some, it is the peace of having close family and friends. For others, it may be the need to face challenges. For them, the give-and-take involved with risk is a driving source for life. What is it that you *need*, not want, to continue surviving? Remember the Havamal's advice on giving too much. We need be aware that we must have something, if not an abundance of it, before we can give it to others. What is that something for you?

ISA, |

Keywords: ice, stasis, absolute zero
Examples: stubbornness, the parts of you that will never change

Isa is the energy of ice. It represents all those things that do not move. There is no change in an environment of stasis, and this is the realm of Isa. The people of Scandinavia have great experience with ice, as their lands are covered by it a good part of the year. It is no wonder that ice made it into the ancient Nordic people's daily mythology.

For us today, the concept of the unchangeable is still persistently relevant. We have many aspects of our daily world that are unchangeable. In the physical nature of our existence, we have many things that will not change. For example, the genetic code of an individual, or his or her familial relations are unchanging.

With the psyche, the part that is Isa may be more difficult to find. Look at the parts of your "you" that have not changed. Do you still speak the same language you did as a child? Is this the language of your thoughts? Are there some areas that you stubbornly refuse to change? These areas are governed by Isa. Keep in mind that every year, the ice thaws, and a new layer will come in the winter. This principle could mean that what is firm and unchanging now may be different in time. Nonetheless, your Isa is what is unchangeable for now.

JERA, ⌖

Keywords: harvest, boon, success of work
Examples: goals you have achieved or will achieve, the things you have today

Jera makes an excellent contrast to the energies of Isa. Where Isa will not move or change, Jera represents the success that comes from an ever-changing world. The ancients were primarily farmers. For them, Jera represented a vital energy. The Jera of harvest provided for (Gebo) the needs (Nauthiz) for the community (Mannaz) to live another year. This boon was not always easy to obtain. It was not granted from gifts or generosity. Rather, to reap the rewards of the harvest, everyone had to labor throughout the growing and harvesting seasons.

For today's society, we may not be as agrarian as our ancestors, but the energy of Jera is still vital to us. Most of us need to work a daily job to receive a paycheck. This paycheck, and the goods purchased with it, are Jera. Interest earned on money or an investment is Jera. The money that exists is being put to use; that use is rewarded through interest.

Tied in with Jera is goal-setting and achievement. Whether we know it or not, we all have goals that we are constantly in the pursuit of. These goals can be as simple as getting up in the morning or taking a walk. They can be as complex as landing a great job or marrying the ideal person. The energy of Jera is that goal. The ancients' goal was a bountiful harvest and an abundance of livestock. The medium of the goals may have changed in today's world, but the concept is still as viable as it ever was.

To find your current Jera, look to what you do have. What is it that you own or that is a part of your character? These are things that you have worked for. Surely, your paycheck helps pay the rent or mortgage on your home. You may have a personal goal that you have achieved. Even a person who no longer jumps at the sight of a spider can find their Jera in their resolve as they shoo the arachnid safely from their home.

EIHWAZ, ᛇ

Keywords: yew tree, mystical experience
Examples: spiritual connection, rooted, psychic abilities

To the ancient peoples of Scandinavia, the yew tree was the tree of the dead. It was found in cemeteries on grave markers to denote the date of death. The legendary world tree, Yggdrasil, was a yew. The Anglo-Saxon rune poem states that the yew is a "joy upon an estate"; the Norwegian rune poem says "it singes when it burns." These references allude to the mystical nature of the yew tree. They reflect the positive and mystical connections associated with the yew.

For an individual, the energy of Eihwaz is that of a person's universal connection. As Yggdrasil connects all worlds, so Eihwaz connects a person to all of the universes. It serves as a reminder of our cosmic roots and the fact that all of us are all a part of everything. You can identify your Eihwaz as how connected you feel to the spiritual realms of the universe.

Ask yourself how connected you are with spiritual matters. Do you feel isolated from the spiritual side of life, or do you have an innate understanding of how spiritual matters work? Remember to look for your answers in that part of you where there are no words. You will see the type and the level of your Eihwaz's reflection deep within. For some, their Eihwaz will be readily apparent—such is the case with mystics and spiritual leaders. Others may not find their own Eihwaz immediately. In this case, simply understand that everyone has Eihwaz energy and that, when the time is right, it will reveal itself.

You can also find your Eihwaz by looking at your psychic abilities. Do you seem to know what is happening or about to happen? Look to any abilities you may have, no matter what they are. They are your Eihwaz connection.

PERTHRO, ㄃

Keywords: fate, the unknowable, luck
Examples: your karma, openness, sense of purpose

The ancient peoples were very aware of their connection with fate. They believed at the moment of birth, one's orlog, or fate, was already set. Since our actions dictate our luck, they also believed we have influence on how we achieve our destinies.

When this energy is applied to the individual, the first place to look for it is in your luck. Do things happen easily for you, or do you have to struggle? Look closer now. You may notice that some things are easier, while others are harder. Even look to what things you find joy in and what things resonate with you. As you begin to identify these things, you see where your fate is leading you.

We all have as a part of our subtle reality a body known as the Hamingja. This Hamingja is that part of us that brings about positive or negative situations. It is the part of us that makes sure we pay off our karmic debts. It is programmed by thoughts, feelings, and actions. It literally creates the You reality about you. When looking at this aspect of yourself, look to how you view the world. You may notice that if you approach it with a pessimistic attitude, negative situations come your way. The energy of the Hamingja is a mirror reflecting your inner energy. The dynamic of this reflection is your Perthro.

ELHAZ, ᛉ

Keywords: elk, protection, higher spiritual vibrations
Examples: divine connection, sense of security, higher spiritual functions

One of the best ways to dispel darker and malevolent forces is not with an equal energy, but with an opposite energy. To fight fire with fire may create a fire twice as big. While the gods had Thor to protect them from the baser elements, he was not their only defense. The energy of the light elves, Vanir, and Aesir is that of higher spiritual vibrations. This is the energy found in higher levels of consciousness, wide-seeing wisdom, and even in unconditional love. Laughter is the highest form of spiritual vibration that can exist within the human body. High-level spiritual energy is poison to beings with negative intent. Thurses may feed on anger, fear, and hatred; they die with unconditional love and laughter. These are the gifts of Elhaz. When they are brought into Midgardh, they clear any negative energy and leave a protected space.

The energy of Elhaz is a stark contrast with Thurisaz. Where Thurisaz is active and destructive, the energy of Elhaz is passive and protective. To find your Elhaz, first ask yourself if there is a place or a time when you find an innate sense of safety. This sense of safety is not something you need to actively promote or produce. It is something that is within you.

Connected with this energy is your higher spiritual function. Where Eihwaz linked you with both the lower and upper worlds, Elhaz connects you only to the upper worlds. The energy of Elhaz connects you to the realm of your higher self. This part of you knows everything about you, throughout all time. This part of you truly knows what is best for you and is there to provide advice when you need it. To further evaluate your Elhaz, look to your connection to these higher spiritual states.

SOWILO, ∫

Keywords: sun, power, striking force
Examples: inner power, motivation

For many ancient cultures the sun was a source of power, divinity, and life. It had the power to melt ice and destroy icebergs. In fact, it was the only thing that could destroy ice. In addition to this strength, the sun possessed the power of life. Sunna, the sun goddess, initiated the return of spring and brought life back to the lifeless soil.

On a physical level, a person's Sowilo is readily apparent. The primary function of the body of any mammal is to produce heat. This function is done at the cellular level. We may only notice it as our body temperature rises after exercise or eating a large meal.

For the psyche, Sowilo is closely associated with the energy of Thurisaz. Both of these runes have very similar qualities: they are dynamic, active, and powerful. However, Sowilo is nurturing and creative, whereas Thurisaz is destructive.

A direct opposite to Isa, Sowilo has the power to break through the stagnation and bring life. What is your driving force? Why do you get up every morning? Where Jera may be your goals, your Sowilo is that inner part of you that pushes you to achieve them. You can see this in the phrases, "It gets my fire going" and "I am all fired up about it." Define the "it," and you will find your Sowilo.

TIWAZ, ↑

Keywords: Tyr, discipline, justice
Examples: self-discipline, putting others first, daily routine

As we have explored, Tyr is the one-handed god who willingly sacrificed his hand so that the forces of chaos and destruction could be bound. This legend of Tyr lived within the hearts of all Nordic warriors. They called on him for protection in battle. It is also this sense of self-sacrifice for the greater good, exemplified by Tyr, that drove the warriors to fight noble battles. We can look at the energy of Thurisaz or Sowilo as the energy of attack and Tiwaz as the parry of that attacking energy.

For the individual, this sense of self-sacrifice can carry over into everyday life. You need not be a soldier or warrior to realize your Tiwaz. The Tiwaz energy is present in the person who puts other people before him- or herself, in any way. It is the motivating force behind the generosity and hospitality of Gebo.

Given the nature of the soldier, Tiwaz is also associated with discipline. This is the energy of routine and following the straight and narrow. Combining the two concepts of self-sacrifice and discipline, we actually see an easy-to-recognize aspect of most peoples' day. The morning routine, taking care of family and home, pursuing a career, or caring for a sick loved one are all examples of where you find your Tiwaz energy.

You will find your Tiwaz within your moral compass, daily routine, and honorable deeds.

BERKANA, ᛒ

Keywords: birch tree, female fertility, fertile lands
Examples: nurturing, your feminine side

The energy of Berkana is something that permeates all cultures through time. To the ancient Norse, this energy was possessed by all of the goddesses. It is female, fertile energy. This energy runs from carnal desires, represented by Freya, to the hearth and home energy of Frigg.

Within the individual, even if it is repressed, there is still a nurturing energy. It may be readily apparent in the care-giving individual. Some may argue that the workaholic, male business executive lacks any Berkana energy. But while the man dedicated to business life may overlook the needs of individuals, he does nurture the needs of the business.

The energy of one's Berkana may also reside outside of the body in the You environment. Every idea, every seed of inspiration, needs a fertile field to grow in, and you may find this fertile ground in your environment. For some, this fertile Berkana ground is created by the give-and-take of personal relationships. You can see your Berkana by noticing what makes you feel cared for, nurtured, and energized. This energy is even more apparent when you return it to the source from which it came, such as friends and family.

EHWAZ, ᛗ

Keywords: horse, movement, status, crossing the worlds
Examples: title, position of power, vehicle, shamanic travel

The existing poems of Ehwaz describe the horse with pride and as a comfort. They also put it in the realm of royalty. People of noble status were buried with their horses, so that they would have an easy means of travel to the underworld. The horse was also used by those skilled at the shamanic arts as a way to reach the underworld.

For everyday life, one's Ehwaz exists within the realm of the You as the vehicle you drive. If you can pilot a plane, boat, or any other sort of vehicle, this ability is part of your Ehwaz. Connected to this mobility is your primary means of getting around. Do you walk, or are you in need of mobility assistance? All forms of movement are viable forms of Ehwaz energy.

Ehwaz also covers social status. We can think of a horse as a status symbol to the ancients. In today's world, expensive sports and luxury cars are status symbols. You can also consider your title at work, your position in a family, your status in your community or in life as your Ehwaz.

MANNAZ, ᛗ

Keywords: mankind, the individual, sentience
Examples: a name, community, gathering of people

All of the runes describe an energy form that was relevant to the ancient people. None of these energies was more relevant to them than that of the people. Without humanity, the wisdom of the runes may not have been fully realized. It took the consciousness that humanity continues to develop to bring runes to the world.

Your Mannaz is, first and simply, found within your name. Beyond this, Mannaz is a reflection of the full extent of the "you" level of yourself. You may not be able to express this aspect of yourself with words. Rather, Mannaz provides you with an abstract concept that ultimately only one person will ever truly know. Some spiritual traditions consider this the power of "I am," devoid of title, rank, or name. You simply are as you are.

While that concept may sound isolating, the energy of Mannaz is not. The energy that is you is also the same energy that is everyone else. You have different combinations of certain aspects. Some aspects may be stronger, others harder to find. Nevertheless, it is the Mannaz energy that combines us all. For that reason, Mannaz takes the "you" placement of its energy and reflects it in the You. You will see this reflection in the company you keep, what sort of neighborhood you live in, and the work environment you have placed yourself in. Your Mannaz, ultimately, is the sum total of your "you" and You.

LAGUZ, ᛚ

Keywords: water, flowing, mysteries
Examples: emotional state, dreams, psychic ability

Samuel Taylor Coleridge once wrote, "water, water, everywhere...." Whether this water is to drink or not, this statement is true for all of life on planet Earth. The ancients knew the value of water to life. They also had a great deal of mythology surrounding all forms of water.

Within the psyche, we need to take into account the metaphorical nature of Laguz. Emotions are typically associated with the element of water. Human emotions tend to reside within the nonverbal parts of the mind. They are one of our connections with the subconscious mind. Deep within the subconscious is where we find dreams. Therefore, your Laguz is your dreams and your emotions.

Look to your self and find what emotions you experience most. Are they happy, sad, angry, positive, or negative? The nature of your Laguz is also tied with your emotional state. You can think of your Laguz as happiness and contentment, anger and upset, or any other combination of energies. Maybe your Laguz is well balanced because you experience and accept all of your various emotional states.

INGUZ, ◇

Keywords: Freyr, seed, male fertile energy
Examples: ideas and concepts, contained energy

Freyr is the twin brother of Freya. They both represent the carnal desires and action of animals that sexually reproduce. The male energy is found within the sperm or seed, while the female energy is found within the womb or fertile field (Berkana). The masculine energy is securely contained until it can be released.

Since the nature of masculine fertile energy is found within a seed, this contained energy is naturally reflected into the male psyche. For example, it may be a basic, natural instinct for men to hide their emotions. To find your Inguz, you can look to the parts of yourself that you may hide or keep repressed. Keep in mind that Inguz is not that part that is contained; rather, it is the action of containment.

Since Inguz has this containment energy, it can also be found with ideas and concepts. Left alone, any idea will go nowhere. You must take your ideas and plant them in some sort of fertile land. These ideas, no matter how small, come from your Inguz energy. You can ask yourself if this energy is abundant or lacking. You may notice that there is a balance between what you keep repressed, mentally and emotionally, and the free flowing of ideas. Take the time to understand this balance.

DAGAZ, ᛞ

Keywords: day, transformation, a 180-degree turn
Examples: changing of mind or emotions, major life changes

With the coming of the day comes the sun. This light is the dispeller of darkness and fear. To the ancients, the return of the sun after the long dark winter meant the melting of ice and a return to the growing season. The ancients described this sense of transformation as the energy of Dagaz.

We all have those parts of us that are unchanging or difficult to change; this is the energy of Isa. The opposite of this energy is Dagaz. Look within and find what parts of you are always changing. Dagaz is not necessarily the energy of growth. Rather, it is the parts of you that experience 180-degree turns. These parts are not always easy to locate, and rarely are they found in the present. But they can be found in your past or even in a planned future.

Was there something that you changed your mind about? Do you now feel completely different than you used to about something? This energy of change is the Dagaz found within your you. The You placement of this energy lies within changes of employment, living situations, or even status. You may have recently gotten married or experienced a loss. These examples are extreme cases in which you can find your Dagaz.

OTHALA, ᛟ

Keywords: inheritance, legacy, nonmoveable wealth
Examples: home, family, genetics, heirlooms

In all cultures, family and the continued existence of the family line are important matters. The ancient people gave the family and its bonds sacred importance. While they did not have family surnames, they passed down the names of parents and ancestors through their descendants. Passed down also were land, riches, stories, and customs.

One of the most visible places to find your Othala is to look to your surname, which ties you in with your family, even if you joined that family by marriage or adoption instead of birth. You can also find your Othala within your genetic structure. Is there a dominant trait or disease that is passed on in your family? Othala can be found within the You realm of existence in any sort of inheritance or heirlooms that are passed down.

You will also be able to find your Othala energy within. Look to the times when you may have heard your parents' words resounding within you. You may also find that you think about and feel the same way about certain topics as your family does. A pilot may still hear a flight instructor's words in his or her mind while landing the plane. All of these examples depict the subtle Othala energy that lives within you.

Exercise 4: Your Inner Futhark

In this exercise you will take stock of yourself from the perspective of the Elder Futhark. Every one of these runes applies to you in some way. It is now your job to find out how. You may find some runes are more prominent than others. You may encounter a rune that does not readily identify itself to you. When this happens, it will require deep, inner contemplative work. Persist, and you will find how the rune applies to you.

Bear in mind that as you approach the middle of the Futhark you will embark on a deep, soul-searching adventure. As you explore Wunjo (ᚹ), Hagalaz (ᚺ), Nauthiz (ᚾ), and Isa (ᛁ), you may start to dig up old skeletons you thought were long dead. As you encounter such things, be willing to take time and apply self-care. You may even need to find outside assistance to help you work through these things. Keep in mind that none of these things are bad or evil, nor do they need to be cast out and destroyed. These are parts of your being as common as an arm. It is how you come to understand, embrace, and finally use these parts of your being that will determine how easily your reality changes. In a sense, Hagalaz, Nauthiz, and Isa are runes of blocks and pitfalls, but they can also be your greatest tools for growth and self-awareness.

A Twenty-four-Point Self-analysis

This self-analysis is the heart of the rest of the work ahead. To truly change your reality, you must know what to change. In order to make the changes, you need to understand the tools you have on hand. For this reason, you are given the opportunity to see yourself in a new light shining through twenty-four different angles.

As you proceed through each of these stages, you will encounter the same three tasks:

1. Each rune will have three simple questions for you to answer.
2. Take the answers from these questions to form a simple statement.
3. Reduce that statement into one or two words.

Feel free to skip around from rune to rune as you feel drawn. You are not expected to undertake all of this process at once. In fact, doing it as a complete routine may muddle the results. Each rune is a unique energy, so take the time to respect each of these aspects about your self. Give each rune its own place and time to let it reveal itself to you. As you finish with one rune, let yourself be done with it. When you move to the next rune, do not let the previous one influence you. Take each rune in its own time and space.

Even though the descriptions of the runes in previous chapters may have used contrasts and comparisons, resist the temptation to compare and contrast the runes during your self-analysis. Allow each inner rune to reveal itself in its own way. Once you have done so, then you may compare or contrast results.

YOUR INNER FUTHARK

===

FEHU, ᚠ: Your Self-value, Your Intrinsic Worth

The concept of self-esteem is of great value to the Fehu rune. Do you feel confident, or shy and hidden? There may even be some part or aspect of yourself that you are most proud of. This part may tie into your view of your own self-value. Look at how other people see you as well. Are you a valuable asset to your place of work or social network? All of these values that are placed upon yourself are the makeup of your Fehu.

1. What is the best thing about you? _____

2. What part of your life are you most proud of? _____

3. What are you good at doing? _____

Summary statement of what is valuable about you: _____

_____

One- to two-word summary: _____

URUZ, ᚢ: Your Strengths

Your physical strength is the first, obvious place to look for your Uruz. What characterizes the strength, health, vitality, and stamina of your physical body? But Uruz is not limited to the physical realm. This area differs greatly from person to person. Some may find that they have strength in their expression of emotions; others may see this ability as a weakness. What is it about you that you consider to be your strengths? You may even look to Fehu. What you perceive to be your value may well be directly tied to what you find to be your strengths.

1. Which is stronger, your physical or emotional strength? _____

2. In what area of your life do you have the most stamina? _____

3. What other strengths do you have? _____

Summary statement of strengths: _____

_____

One- to two-word summary: _____

Thurisaz, ᚦ: Your Dynamic Energy

How aggressive are you? How easy is it for you to start things and be diligent? While Thurisaz has the nature to be violent, that may or may not be your nature. You may find your Thurisaz in the quickness of your temper or your quickness to defend youself. Or you may find your Thurisaz in how passionately you pursue your goals. The nature of Thurisaz, ultimately, is of dynamic energy. What is it, deep in your nature, that really gets you going?

1. How easily are you angered? _____

2. What makes you defensive? _____

3. What is your driving force in life? _____

Summary statement of how your energy is thrust into the world: _____

_____

One- to two-word summary: _____

ANSUZ, ᚨ: Your Ability to Communicate and Understand

Think of your best methods of communicating. How is it that you best understand the world and yourself? You can first look to how easily you learn things. Is there a special subject at which you excel? You can also look at your outpouring of information. Do you find it easy to talk about certain subjects? Maybe it is not even a subject that makes it easy for your talk, but rather the environment you're in. You may find your Ansuz energy lies with public speaking, conversing with friends, or creating some great work of art on your own. To understand your Ansuz is to understand that part of you that easily accepts and transmits information.

1. Is there a subject that has been easy for you to learn? _____

2. What do you find easy to talk about? _____

3. Do you prefer talking to large or small groups or to individuals?

_____

Summary statement of where you easily receive and give information:

_____

_____

One- to two-word summary: _____

RAIDO, ᚱ: Your Mobility, How You Move and Travel

The first place to look for your Raido is with your primary means of mobility. Do you walk? Do you use a wheelchair or a cane? In addition, look to your primary and preferred means of transportation. Do you ride a bicycle, drive a car, or fly a plane? How you prefer to move about, at what speeds, and with what level of ease is your Raido energy.

1. How do you get around? _____

2. Do you move fast or slowly? _____

3. When you travel, how do you prefer to go? _____

Summary statement of how you get about: _____

_____

One- to two-word summary: _____

KENNAZ, ᚲ: Your Creativity

What talents or skills do you possess? What is your personal creative strength? It can be anything from housecleaning to doing math to creating artwork. Look to what comes easiest to you. If you find that you are struggling with something but have a passion for it, your Thurisaz may be out of sync with your Kennaz. This discrepancy is not a problem—merely an indication of a new skill to develop. Keeping that in mind, one's Kennaz is not always static. As you promote and improve the energies of your Ansuz, you may find that you gain new talents and skills. These changes are the evolution of your Kennaz nature. Simply look at what you do well, and you will see Kennaz.

1. What skills or talents do you have? _____

2. Do you find creativity flows easily, or do you have to work at it?

_____

3. In what areas in your life are you the most creative?

_____

Summary statement of how you are creative: _____

_____

One- to two-word summary: _____

GEBO, ✕: Your Generosity, Your Willingness to Give and Take

Give-and-take is the essential part of Gebo. Are you able to receive gifts as easily as you give them, or do you find it hard to give and easy to receive? There is some sense of flow associated with the Gebo energy. Really look to see how hard you have to push yourself in order to give to others. This is not a sign of a defect or flaw. Rather, if you are finding it difficult to give to others, maybe you have chance to learn to first give to yourself. Remember, a gift demands a gift. You improve your Gebo energy by giving to yourself. As you do, you may find this energy easily beginning to flow to others. Only a full cup can fill others.

1. Do you give freely? _____

2. Can you receive gifts easily? _____

3. What sorts of things are easier for you to give and receive? _____

_____

Summary statement of what you give and receive and how easy it is:

_____

_____

One- to two-word summary: _____

WUNJO, ᚹ: Your Joy

How happy are you? What is your capacity for joy? There is something that makes you happy in some way. There is something in the world that gives you some sense of comfort or pleasure. This something is reflected within your being as your Wunjo. We all have it. This section will invariably have its pitfalls and upheavals. You may feel guilt for being happy, or there may be many things that get in the way of you being happy. If these things come up, do not list them here; save them for Hagalaz. All you want to do here is to be joyful in the moment. Give yourself permission to feel and list all of those things that make you happy. Now look to what they have in common: this is your Wunjo.

   1. What makes you happy? _____

   2. How often are you happy? _____

   3. What brings you peace and comfort? _____

Summary statement of what brings you happiness, peace, and comfort most

often: _____

_____

One- to two-word summary: _____   _____

HAGALAZ, ᚺ: Your Turmoil and Strife (Both Internal and External)

What struggles do you have with yourself? As seen with Wunjo, these are the things that could get in the way of your happiness. These are the little demons that we all have that sabotage our best-laid plans. Deep within our psyche hide the negative things that were once said. These are the things we keep telling ourselves, and we believe them. You may not even be aware that these things are created internally. Are there certain events that keep happening in your life? Just as you can with all the other runes, you can use this revelation as a mirror to discover deeper parts of your self that you may never knew even existed.

1. What causes you the most anguish in your life? _____

2. In what areas do you easily fall apart? _____

3. What specific areas do your voices of doubt and denial speak of?

_____

Summary statement of areas in your life where there is upheaval:

_____

One- to two-word summary: _____

NAUTHIZ, ᚾ: Your Needs

What do you need to live? With physical needs, Nauthiz is easy. We need food, water, shelter, and medicine, for example. What are your physical and material needs? Do you have great emotional needs? Nauthiz is not things you want, but things necessary for your survival. Where Thurisaz helped you to have passion and drive, Nauthiz may be that which holds you back. When you dig deep inside, you will discover you have needs that are as vital to your emotional and spiritual well-being as air and water are to your physical well-being. These needs are not things to be shunned or repressed. Rather, you must embrace and understand this part of your character. The energy of Nauthiz is also that which you need to do before you can move on. Nauthiz is like a debt in need of payment.

1. What are your greatest physical needs? _____

_____

2. What are your greatest emotional needs? _____

_____

3. What blocks you from fulfilling your needs? _____

Summary statement of what you need and what stops your needs from being

sated: _____

_____

One- to two-word summary: _____

ISA, |: Your Stability

How grounded are you? What part of you never changes? Perhaps your face
and body shape have become stable. When losing weight or gaining muscle,
you can reach plateaus that may be thought of as Isa energy.

What about your emotional stability? Are there situations in which you
are rock solid? Are you solid all the time or only when needed? Keep in mind
that stoicism may actually be a repression of emotions. If so, this repression
is Isa. You have locked into stasis all the memories, feelings, and thoughts you
feel are not appropriate. Just like the sun rises again at the end of night, so
too do these things resurface. Better to face them now, while you are calm and
ready, than in an unexpected situation.

1. What never changes about you? _____

2. What do you hide from the world? _____

3. What part of you is rock solid and steady? _____

_____

Summary statement about what is stable and solid within you:

_____

_____

One- to two-word summary: _____

JERA, ⟨: Your Success

What have you accomplished? What are you going to accomplish? What is your greatest potential? Jera is that which you have earned and continue to earn. You can think of this as your paycheck, position with a company, or place in a community. Jera need not be relegated to external rewards. You may have many internal achievements: stopping smoking, losing weight, overcoming a phobia, or even just allowing yourself to be free with your emotions. Think about all those little things that you have won and that added up to the greater successes, and you will have a good stock of your Jera.

1. What have you accomplished? _____

2. What do you have that shows your success? _____

_____

3. In what internal areas have you been successful? _____

_____

Summary statement of what you have accomplished or what you easily achieve:

_____

One- to two-word summary: _____

EIHWAZ, ↓: Your Completeness

What is your spiritual connection? Do you feel well rooted in a spiritual tradition, or do you float to whatever works best for you? Just as Isa can ground and calm, Eihwaz also can have a sense of being rooted. If you have found yourself living in one place for a long time, you may notice that you are tightly woven into the fabric of the community. You can extend this perspective to the emotional and spiritual realms as well.

For your emotional Eihwaz, determine how complete your range of emotions is. Are you accepting of your darker side just as much as your lighter side? Emotions are deeply rooted to the spiritual energies; are you aware of your ability to traverse through the lower, middle, and upper realms?

On a spiritual level, you can assume your Eihwaz is that which takes you from the depths of the underworlds to the heights of upper worlds.

1. How well do you feel both your darker parts and lighter parts? ________

____

2. In what life area are you most rooted? ____________________

3. What about you do you feel is the most complete? ____________

____

Summary statement of how and where you feel you are a complete being:

____

____

One- to two-word summary: ______________________________

PERTHRO, ᛈ: Your Fate, Your Luck

Look at the events in your life. Do things work out easily, or are things more difficult? Do these events seem to pull you in a specific direction? The Norse believed that all things were tied together by the weavings of the Norns. For this reason, all things that happened were fated to happen. So, too, are the events in your life. But you still have decision-making powers. If things move smoothly in an area of your life, you may find that you have positive feelings about it. A person who finds many obstacles and a constantly downward-spiraling life may be filled with negative thoughts. To understand your Perthro is to understand your luck and how you are connected to its execution.

1. What area of your life moves easiest? ____________________

2. What part is the most difficult? ________________________

3. What seems to be the overall direction of your life? __________

____

Summary statement of how and in what area of your life your luck is

manifesting: _____

_____

One- to two-word summary: _____

ELHAZ, Ⲩ : Your Spiritual Nature

Elhaz is the divine/spiritual energy of your being. It is the flow of the higher spiritual energies through your being. Look to the times you spend in peaceful repose. Does this happen often or rarely? Elhaz is your ability to manifest the upper-world energies and bring them into reality. It is also your ability to feel secure. It is not the sense of security that active measures bring. Rather, this sense of security comes from the confidence that you do not have to actively protect yourself. Is there some part of your being or home that enjoys this state?

A caution does come with Elhaz and protection. If Elhaz is too strong and used too much, the energy will turn into Isa energy and lock up that which it was once meant to protect.

1. In what area in your life do you have the most security? _____

_____

2. When, where, and how do you feel the most safe? _____

_____

3. What are the circumstances in which you feel a strong connection with the

divine? _____

Summary statement of when you are safe in your spiritual element:

_____

_____

One- to two-word summary: _____

SOWILO, ⚡: Your Energetic Nature

How do you use and give off energy? Are you vibrant and outgoing? How much charisma do you have? Your Sowilo energy is the impact you have in the world around you. Look to see if you are quiet and shy or if you let your light shine upon all things around you. Where Isa locks up and represses, Sowilo unleashes to the world. Where, in your world, do you shine the most? This is where your Sowilo energy is the strongest. Sometimes a famous performer's Sowilo is vibrant and alive on stage, but their personality hides behind Isa when it comes to one-on-one meetings. You may find your Sowilo and Isa to be polar opposites. You can use your Sowilo to overcome the challenges of your Isa.

1. When are you the most outgoing? _____

2. What situations bring you to life? _____

3. What do you have a drive or passion for? _____

Summary statement of how your energy is raised and manifested in the world:

_____

_____

One- to two-word summary: _____

TIWAZ, ↑: Your Discipline

How focused and disciplined are you? Can you stay on task? Do you have a steady routine that you follow? Your Tiwaz can be found in many areas of your life. It is found easily with your regular routine. Do you follow the same pattern daily? If so, you are starting to find your Tiwaz.

Associated with Tiwaz is your moral compass. Are you the type of person who always strives to do what you think is right? Do you defend the rights of others? Just as everything can be taken to the extremes and used ignobly, so can Tiwaz. One's morality can be forced upon others to the point where Tiwaz becomes tyranny.

There is a direct connection with the status of your Tiwaz and the alignment of your Perthro. As you live nobly, your Perthro will become positive, and your luck improves.

1. In what area of life do you find easiest to stay on task? _____

_____

2. How strongly do you follow your own morality or that of your community?

_____

3. How do you define the majority of your deeds? _____

_____

Summary statement of how strong you follow your own straight-and-narrow:

_____

_____

One- to two-word summary: _____

BERKANA, ᛒ: Your Fertility, Your Manifestation of Ideas, Your Potential

Do you accomplish what you set out to do? We all are wide-open vestiges, able to manifest anything we see fit to bring about. Knowing this, take a look at what you manifest in the world about you. Are you living the life you wish to? What are you doing to manifest it? What is it, exactly, that you are bringing into your life? Is it wealth and happiness or frustration and debt? If you don't like what you bring into the world, then you can grow a different crop. The first step is to understand what it is you bring about and why. You are already taking that first step when you honestly take stock in the nature of your Berkana.

1. What sort of things manifest easily in your life? _____

_____

2. How would you describe the nature of those things? _____

_____

3. Which of your ideas and plans are easily realized? _____

_____

Summary statement of how your potential is manifested in the world:

_____

_____

One- to two-word summary: _____

EHWAZ, M: Your Social Status

Where do you fit into the world and your communities? How do you define yourself to others? Quite often, your Jera leads you to your Ehwaz. What is your title at work? Where do you fit in with the community? By answering these questions, you will find where your Ehwaz is the best fit. Often, it is the place where you have focused more of your time and energy. It is also the area that your have had the best feelings about. That which you give to positively, grows positively.

However, just because one has the title and position of manager, doesn't mean he or she feels like a manager. This is the dichotomy of Ehwaz. One may bear the title but not feel the responsibility. On the other hand, when you behave like you have the status you wish to achieve, you often attain it.

1. What title or rank do you bear? _____

2. How do others see your place in society? _____

_____

3. What level of status do you feel you have or could easily achieve?

_____

Summary statement of your place in society (where it is, where you feel it is, or where others see it):

_____

_____

One- to two-word summary: _____

MANNAZ, ᛗ: You, the Person

What is your name? Who are you really? Where Ehwaz is your social identity, Mannaz is your personal identity—the person you and those who have an intimate understanding of you see. Where Ehwaz offered the placement of rank and title, Mannaz gets to the heart of who you really are.

Mannaz, put simply, is your birth name or the name others call you regularly. Mannaz is a leveler of the playing field. Ehwaz places you in various positions of power; Mannaz reminds you that we all are human. We all have the same needs and deserve the same respect. Ehwaz asks, what are you? Mannaz asks, who are you?

1. What is your name? _____

2. What other means do you use to identify yourself? _____

_____

3. What do you have in common with everyone else? _____

_____

Summary statement of who you are: _____

_____

_____

One- to two-word summary: _____

LAGUZ, ᛚ: Your Depth

What are your dreams and inner visions? How easily are you able to flow with situations? Are you firm and rigid with everything in life? Or are you laid-back, taking things as they come? We all have a depth of character, but this depth can be found in different places with different people. Look to the areas you feel that you have taken a deep dive into. For some, this area may be art or science. What is it that you know a great deal about or even have a great passion for? This is where you will find your Laguz. It will be in this area in your life that you see the manifestation of your dreams. Because of this depth and connection, you may even find your psychic abilities linked here. If so, your Laguz has a psychic connection.

1. What do you have a passion for? _____

2. How does this passion show itself? _____

_____

3. What do you feel strongly about? _____

Summary statement of the areas in which you have depth and how your depth

reaches the world: _____

_____

One- to two-word summary: _____

INGUZ, ◇: Your Spark, the Seed of Your Desires

What part of you is locked away but needs to manifest? This part of your potential success is what you pair with Berkana to achieve Jera. If Isa is that which locks and hides away, Inguz is that which stores. Inguz is that part of you that is waiting to manifest into the real world. It is your success potential. It can be found in your ideas, dreams, and aspirations. Because your Berkana may not be the best place to plant certain seeds, many of these great potential things may not happen. But with the awareness of your Inguz, you will identify how your Berkana can change to achieve your successes.

1. In what areas do you find you have the most ideas? _____

_____

2. Do your plans take long to realize, or do they just grow?

_____

3. What ideas or plans do you have waiting to be realized?

_____

Summary statement of how easily your desires can be realized:

_____

_____

One- to two-word summary: _____

DAGAZ, ᛞ: Your Ever-changing Parts

What parts of you—physical, emotional, mental, or otherwise—always change? What area or areas in your life are always in the process of change and evolution? Is it easy for you to change your mind and opinions on things? Do you change your dressing style or the style of music you like? The accomplishment of your dreams is Dagaz in motion. Are your ready for a great success? What is it, within you or around you, that is about to become real? Are you a budding musician looking to make it big, or are you looking to get a promotion at work? As you find the cusp of change—any sort of change—you will find where your Dagaz energy lies.

1. What parts of your being are always changing? _____

_____

2. What area of your life is about to be realized? _____

_____

3. How often do changes happen? _____

Summary statement of what is changing about you and will soon to come to

light: _____

_____

One- to two-word summary: _____

OTHALA, ᛟ: Your Assets

What do you have that came from your family? What is your inheritance and your genetic makeup? Fehu represents your subjective value, or what you offer to society; your Othala is what has been granted to you from birth. Your Fehu may contain elements from your Othala. A person may see his or her value within the entertainment they give from writing music. This talent with music may have been inherited from parents who are equally skilled in music.

Internally, look to what skills you have grasped that you will never lose. Really assess what it is that you have that you cannot lose. Just as we pass on genes from one generation to the next, we also pass our attitudes, knowledge, and understandings. Therefore, your Othala may include feelings, beliefs, and ways of acting that resemble those of your elders. Do you act, feel, or believe in the same ways as others in your family? Do you have the same physical attributes, strengths, or illnesses?

1. What do you believe that you have gained from your family and upbringing? _____

2. What are you passing on to others about you? _____

_____

3. When you die, what will people most remember about you?

_____

Summary statement of how who you are affects the world around you:

_____

_____

One- to two-word summary: _____

USING THE RUNES

By now, you have explored the runic energies in three ways: You have seen how the energy was understood in Scandinavia over a thousand years ago. Then you found how the runes exist within all things around you. Finally, you found how the runic energy exists and functions within your being on all levels. In this chapter, we will explore the ways the ancient people used the runes and how you can use them today.

The runes are not just simply energies used for exploring and understanding. Surely they were and still are used for these reasons, but that is not where the runes' power ends. They are also potent tools of transformation. Those skilled in runes were once called upon to help with any sort of situation that the people faced. There are tales of runes used for healing, battle, protection, birth, travel, and more.

It is best to keep in mind that the runes are tools. Their energies may be likened to the energy of a living being with a single thought. The runes have the ability to draw, repel, or even modify their specific energies. There is a caution, of course: the runes are needful when needed and useful when used. This caution is to remind us that the runes are tools, not "fix-it-alls," as they can only influence the subtle layers of reality. This means we can do as we will with the runic energies and still nothing will happen. We can make many amulets, sing rune songs, or write out complex scripts to no avail. Why?

Runes are only tools that use a resource of energy. A house cannot be built simply by the accumulation of tools and resources. It takes the active use of these tools with the materials to construct the house. The same is true with the runes. When effectively used, they will modify the energies of the subtle realities. It is then up to us, in the physical reality, to bring about this energy in a real way.

Let's say a person is intent on winning the lottery. He can do all manner of spells to boost his luck, but if he never goes out of his home to purchase a lottery ticket, he will never win. Likewise, if you use the runes to help you to get a promotion at work, your potential of getting the job is enhanced. At this point, you need to apply for the position and do the work necessary in the physical reality to accomplish your goal.

Sometimes the "getting out and going" is the most challenging part. Knowing what to do or finding the motivation may be the challenge. Since the runes are a part of every level of our existence, they will help with these challenges as well.

Galdr: Singing the Runes

While simply saying the sounds of the runes, or even their names, will suffice, there is a way to bring forth more energy from the sounds you make. In order to do this, you must learn where those energies reside within yourself. Once you have tapped into this energy source, you need to allow this energy to resound and reverberate throughout your being. Then your entire being begins to pulse with the energetic rhythm of the rune. As this energy starts to surge, it will pour out into the world about you, and the realities begin to change in very subtle but powerful ways.

Just as a journey of a thousand miles starts with the first step, galdring starts with a breath. Simple yet elegant, the breathing of the Galdr comes from the belly. Belly breathing tells the body to do many things. A breath from the belly instantly calms you. It brings you out of a fight-or-flight setting. It also slows the processes of the mind so you can begin to focus on one thing at a time. Belly breathing is also healthy, as it stops the flow of stress chemicals and allows the body to begin to produce relaxation hormones. Galdring is a spiritual and meditative action. The mind, body, and emotions must be calmed and centered. It all simply starts with a breath.

To help you get into the groove of belly breathing, put your hand on your stomach. Notice how it rises and falls gently. The rhythm of breathing that you want to establish before galdring is that of an exhale that is twice as long as your inhale. For example, breathe in to the count of four or five (whichever is most comfortable to you), then exhale to the count of eight or ten.

Do nine breaths this way. Nine is a sacred number to the runes, and nine breaths will help further orient yourself into the right runic energy space.

As you breathe, you may find it gets easier to take longer and deeper breaths. When this happens, you are ready for the next step: intoning the runes.

The runic languages and modern English have something in common: vowels in every word. If you look at the names of the runes, you will notice there are two or three vowels in each one. This fact gives you a map that can be used to chart the vibrational energies of the runes within your body. The first step is to identify the vibration of each vowel there.

There are seven vowel runes in the Elder Futhark. Below is a table of these seven runic vowels, their sounds, and an example of their phonetic values found in the English language.

RUNE	SOUND	EXAMPLE
I	*ee* (long *e*)	green
M	*ay* (long *a*)	pay
ᛁ	*eye* (long *i*)	light
ᚠ	*ah* (short *a*)	cha-cha
ᛇ	*y*	year
ᛟ	*oh* (long *o*)	toe
ᚢ	*oo*	tube

Now, take the first runic vowel, Isa (ᛁ), and begin to intone it. Take in a deep belly breath of four or five counts, and as you exhale, intone the i sound (ee). Let it begin to resound within your body and notice where it resonates within.

Many people have found that Isa resonates well at the top of the head. This placement may make sense, as the sound is of a higher frequency pitch-wise. The higher the vibration of the tone, the higher its placement will be within the body. As you move through the vowels, you may notice that each will resound in a different place within your body. For example, many people remark that the *oo* sound of Uruz (ᚢ) resounds deep within the lower parts of the abdomen. Here is a diagram of where the sounds of the runic vowels tend to resound for most people.

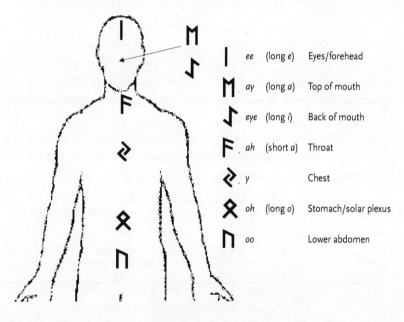

ᛁ	ee	(long *e*)	Eyes/forehead
ᛗ	*ay*	(long *a*)	Top of mouth
ᛃ	eye	(long *i*)	Back of mouth
ᚠ	*ah*	(short *a*)	Throat
ᛉ	*y*		Chest
ᛟ	oh	(long *o*)	Stomach/solar plexus
ᚢ	*oo*		Lower abdomen

Vowel resonations within the body

Take some time to explore each of these vowel sounds and how they resonate within you. After you have discovered the placement of the vowel sounds within you, you can work to resonate that area even more. Then you can move that resonation into the area about you.

To move that resonation outward, you must learn to use your diaphragm to push the air out. You are already breathing using your belly, so a diaphragm push is not going to be a stretch. To understand how it feels to use your diaphragm, say the sounds of the letter s—*sssssssssss*. Notice how as you push out the air you feel a tightness coming from your abdomen. This tightness comes from your diaphragm pushing the air out. This is the part of your body that you want to use to fill the room with your vowel sound.

To start, use the Uruz (ᚢ) sound—*oo*. Take in a long deep breath. As you exhale, feel the vibration resonating within you. Notice the resonation and the feeling you get from it. Next, project the sound into the room around you using your diaphragm. Notice how the sound fills the room. Do not worry if it does not seem to take effect right away. Making the sound resonate in the room may need a bit of practice. With practice, even the smallest of speaking voices can fill a room.

Keep in mind you are not making sounds to resemble anyone else's voice. You have your own voice, your own range, and your own limitations. Do not push yourself to a place where your voice is not ready to go. If you have always spoken quietly, do not try to be as loud or projecting as a trained singer is—at least not right away. You can work your way up to that. Remember, as working with the runes is a deeply personal process, so too is the execution of the work.

After you have the basics with a single vowel, you can start to change vowel sounds. Start with switching from the sounds of *ee* (ᛁ) to *ay* (ᛖ). The sound of Isa will resonate at the top of the head, bringing in the higher-resonating energy. As you change the vowel to the sound of Ehwaz, notice how the resonation actually moves through your head to the top of your mouth. Repeat this intonation process until the change is smooth and you can fill the room with the changes in energy.

Continue to experiment with this process for various changes in vowels. Here are some vowel changes found in runic names:

eh-ah	Jera ⟨, Elhaz Y, Ehwaz M
eh-oh	Gebo X, Perthro K
ee-ah	Isa l
oh-ee-oh	Sowilo ʃ
ah-oo	Ansuz ᚠ, Laguz ᚱ

When intoning the vowel changes and the names of the runes, notice the vertical flow of energy. Moving from *a* to *u* produces a deep, descending movement of energy. Hence, it is appropriate that this change happens within the rune name Laguz (ᚱ). It takes you from conscious awareness in your head to your feelings (deep in the abdomen). Ansuz is another rune that has the same flow of energy, but in a different way. Ansuz represents conscious awareness, while Laguz represents unconscious feelings.

Other runes that have a descending connection with their energy are Fehu (ᚠ), Raido (R), Gebo (X), Perthro (K), and Inguz (◇). Be sure to note just how the energy flows as you intone each of these runes. Allow yourself to be aware of the feelings inside your body, as well as any emotions that stir or psychic impressions that arise. All are important to note.

Three runes—Thurisaz (ᚦ), Nauthiz (ᚾ), Othala (ᚨ)—move energy in an upward direction. Thurisaz can be thought of as manifesting a base energy into the world. Hence, moving upward is an appropriate flow for its energy. Nauthiz is actually a combination of three vowels—*a*, *u*, and *i*. The *a* and *u* act as one sound that starts in the lower part of the abdomen—*ow*. The *ee* sound sends the energy to the top of the head. This shift can be thought of as bringing the needs of the flesh to the attention of the conscious mind, as well as to the spiritual being.

The runes with horizontal energies are interesting studies in contrast. These runes include Uruz with its double *u*'s. This combination stays low in the body, right about the base chakra. Surely this position is a reflection of the rune's primal nature. Hagalaz (ᚻ), Mannaz (ᛗ), and Dagaz (ᛞ) all have horizontal movement about the vowel Ansuz (ᚨ), or the *ah* sound. Each of these runes has a unique energy and understanding about it, yet their energy movement is the same.

The names of the remaining runes have a slight wobble to their energy movements. They move within just a small range. The sounds of some of these runes, such as Jera (ᛃ), Berkana (ᛒ), and Ehwaz (ᛗ), hover about the head. Wunjo's (ᚹ) sounds stay in the lower part of the body. Perhaps this placement is appropriate, as Wunjo is the emotion of joy and settles deep within one's self. This small wobble makes it easy to latch on to its reverberation energy and project it.

One rune that has an extreme wobble is Sowilo. Its sound start slow in the body, on *oh* (ᛋ), moves to the top of the head with *ee* (ᛁ), and finally drops to the base again with *oh* (ᛋ). This dramatic shift in sound and vibration is representative of Sowilo's highly energetic state. Just as the sun rises and falls, so too do the sounds of Sowilo.

The varying sounds of the vowels of the runes give their names a singsong nature. It was said that if you knew the words of Old Norse songs, you knew the melody. There may be a string of truth here, if we follow the frequency vibrations of the vowel sounds. *Ee* (ᛁ), at the top of the head, would have a high-pitched sound. *Oo* (ᚢ), at the base of the abdomen, would have a lower note. Work your way through the sounds of the runes using these changing notes. You will quickly see how they can be made into a song. Experiment by putting together several runes and seeing what sort of a song you can make up.

This action of making a song out of the runes will make it easier for you to remember the runes and their order. The subconscious remembers things better if it can find a pattern or attach some significance to it. The singsong nature of the runes you choose to work with will engrain their meanings and feelings even more deeply into your subconscious. Therefore, to access those runes, all you have to do is sing your rune song, and their energies will easily come to life from a place deep within your being.

Now that you know how to make the rune sounds and project them, it is time to put the actual rune energy to use. This is the part where your visualization skills will come into effect. As you state the name of a rune and follow its vowel changes, picture the energy actually flowing. If the rune's energy flow is horizontal, visualize the shape of the rune as if it were on a plate, growing larger and larger. If the energy moves up a great distance, then visualize its energy like a fountain of runes gushing forth from within you. Contrarily, if the rune's energy descends greatly, visualize it as a waterfall of runes pouring out from the lower part of your being and filling the room. There is no end to the creative imagery you can connect with the movement of runic energy.

Creating Physical Runes

After you have gotten the runic meditations down pat and you have developed your own deep understanding of the runes, the next thing you can do is to create your own working set of runes. These staves will provide homes for the runic energies that you draw to you. Just like the human soul, runic energy requires a body to maintain a permanent existence in the physical world. Then the runes will become strong tools to aid you in your transformation process.

The shape of a rune is appropriately called the stave. It is important to differentiate between the runes and their staves. The runes are not their physical shapes. Instead, the rune is the energy that fills the wood or stone that the shape is carved into. The stave form serves to remind humans what that rune's energy is. It helps us to tune into a rune's energy without the guesswork needed to discern that energy.

This energy contained in the staves serves to tune our own energy system to that of the runes, so that when we need to access the runic energies, they are readily available. The staves are only tools that we can use to draw on runic energies. Ultimately, we need to do the heavy lifting.

Carving Staves

One of the most common ways that the ancients accessed the energies of runes was to carve their staves. There are many artifacts bearing runic scripts. The most common are the large rune stones found all over Scandinavia. There are countless examples of shipping tags, miscellaneous items, and weapons that include runes on them. Magical amulets (called bracteates) and rings with nearly undecipherable scripts have been found. The carvings on these items were used for communicating everything from secret messages to various types of magic spells.

Carving the staves yourself is the ideal way to create your runes, because it gives you a chance to form a strong bond and affinity with your runes. It also ensures that you can load them with your specific understanding of the runic energies. If you cannot carve a set, you may buy a starter set. If necessary, you can even write the staves on a piece of paper. As long as you have staves in some physical form, some kind of physical bodies, for the runes' energies, the runes will work. The writings of Tacitus suggest the ideal medium for carving runes is the wood of a fruit- or nut-bearing tree. Ash, oak, and yew are popular woods for rune carving.

When carving staves, work on one shape at a time. The carving should be done in two simple steps. First carve the main vertical lines of the stave, then carve the smaller, nonvertical ones. As you carve, focus on the energy you have come to understand for the rune you are carving. You can even intone the name of the rune and say the words you know are associated with it. It is important to work on one rune at a time, so the energy does not cross-contaminate to other staves.

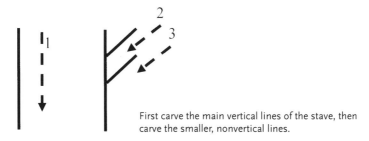

First carve the main vertical lines of the stave, then carve the smaller, nonvertical lines.

Preparing to Load the Staves

After the staves have been carved, they need to be loaded. Loading is simply taking the runic energy, passing it through you, and putting it into the runes.

While loading, you may also take the extra step of staining the runes. Traditionally, staining was done with blood. Using their own blood helped rune carvers get even closer to the energies of the runes. The runes they carved were truly born of them, physically and spiritually. Today, staining with blood may not be the most desirable method. Many people use red ochre or even red paint. Others still choose to incorporate a part of themselves into the runes in different ways. Follow how you feel led.

The loading process is sacred and spiritual. Sometimes this type of action could open one to undesirable energies. For this reason, it is recommended that you load your staves while in a protected space. Setting up this space is as important as the loading itself, because clearing the space also clears and trains your consciousness to accept only the intended energies.

It is very common to clear a space by lighting candles and incense. Many choose to use white candles. Incense can be any sort that you feel comfortable with. For clearing and setting up sacred space, a mixture of sandalwood, frankincense, myrrh, and copal works very well. If all you can find is stick incense, sandalwood is the best.

A modern space-clearing ritual specific to the Norse traditions is the hammer rite. The hammer of Thor was used to bless and protect everything from birth to death. It was even used to protect the home. To do the hammer rite, face each of the four directions and draw the shape of Thor's hammer— an upside-down capital *T*—in the air. If you have an actual hammer, hold it and use it to "draw" the shape. If you don't have one, just use your hand.

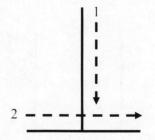

The hammer sign

Now you want to load this space with protective energies. You can do this with a deity invocation: simply call the name of a god or goddess and ask him or her to be present. The best deities for rune work are Thor, for protecting the space, and Odin, for helping guide you through the rune-loading process. You may also choose to invoke ancestors or protective spirits you are already familiar with. (The process for calling spirits is the same as invoking a deity.) It is very common to offer a bowl of mead or other such offering to the deity or spirits you have called.

Now you may begin the actual loading process. This process is known as the alu formula.

Loading the Runes: The Alu Formula

Alu is a word that many runic statements end with. Its exact meaning is debatable. Many say that it means "ale" and represents the spirit of that drink. It is with alcoholic beverages that the ancients saw the world as being imbued with magic and mystery. It is no wonder these beverages are sometime called "spirits." No matter what the definition of alu is, its function is to manifest into reality the statement that precedes it.

The acronym *ALU* also serves as a great mnemonic for remembering the process of loading runes. Each of the three runes that makes up the word *alu*—Ansuz (ᚨ), Laguz (ᛚ), and Uruz (ᚢ)—represents one of the three steps of the loading process.

Before beginning, take a breath to clear yourself of any remaining energies. Then follow these three steps, each centering around the breath.

Step One: Ansuz (ᚨ), Attention
Ansuz deals with the functions of the mind. The first step in the loading process is to know what rune you are using. You focus upon the rune's name and function.

First, inhale. As you do, you will draw a neutral universal energy into your being. Now exhale and sing the name of the rune you are working with. Let yourself feel the rune's energy as you sing its name. As you sing the rune and feel its energy, the energy of your being becomes tuned to the same energy as the rune.

Step Two: Laguz (ᛚ), Letting Energy Flow

In this step, you move the tuned energy into the stave form. Laguz is a rune of flow, and flow is the key to this step. If you ever try to push energy, it will stop. Energy must not be pushed or forced. It seems to know where to go, and if you trust it, it will go there. Let it flow out with your breath, it knows what to do and where to go.

For the second step, as you inhale, allow the rune's energy inside you to "bunch up" around your shoulders and the top of your arms. As you exhale, again sing the name of the rune. As you do, let this rune's energy flow down your arms, through your hands, and into the rune stave that has been carved. Imagine it as a stream of water effortlessly flowing downhill into a lake.

If you choose to color the runes as you load them, do the staining at this step to embed the energy within the layers of the stain and wood. As you exhale, paint the stain upon the stave. Use additional breaths as you apply all the necessary stain.

There is always risk of diluting or altering the energy with new thoughts. This is why it is best to do this step of the loading with one breath. If you feel you need more than one breath to fully flow the energy into the rune, you may take more than one. These subsequent breaths will reinforce the energy of the stave. However, do not draw in any more neutral universal energy as you inhale. To ensure you can do this, keep your thoughts and feelings focused singularly on the one rune's purpose in your working.

Step Three: Uruz (ᚢ), Use

With this step you pull away from the runic energy. Again, trust the energy to do its thing. Once it is in the stave, it needs to come alive. This step is analogous to a baby taking its first breath. Up until the point of birth, a baby received all it needed from its mother. When it takes its first breath, it sets itself as an individual who is starting to grow independently of its mother. As you are the parent of this rune, you need to separate from it and let it grow. This is why Uruz represents this step of the process. Not only does Uruz have the energy of initiation, it also has the energy of strength and vitality.

Inhale to pull your self away from the rune and stave; as you exhale, intone the rune's name again to bring the rune alive in its new body.

• • •

After you have separated from the now-living rune, take a breath to clear your body of the present runic energy. Gather in any remaining energy as you inhale; then, as you exhale, push it out through your feet into the Earth. This breath grounds you and readies you to be filled with the energy of the next rune. The staves must be loaded one at a time, using all three steps of the *alu* formula, in order, before going on to the next, to prevent cross-contamination of energy.

Unless you are very adept at energy work, it is not best to load all of the runes at once. Processing the energy of twenty-four runes in one sitting will be very taxing even for those who have worked with the runes for years. It is best to do no more than four at a time until you are used to the process.

You may thank your protecting deities or spirits and ask them to go, if you please. With rune work, it is not always necessary to ground and close the space. Because you will have cleared the energy after each rune, there will be no residual energies. But the energy of the clearing is still sacred and protective. This energy cannot be broken or destroyed. You may keep it if you wish. Of course, if you feel more comfortable clearing it, you may. Most runic practitioners that work in this way do not find a need to clear space. They just do a simple thanking of their deity as they pour the mead out upon the ground.

When you have finished, gather your now-loaded rune staves into a bag or box for safekeeping.

Bind Runes

The runic energies, while individual in nature, work well together. The way they relate can be thought of as the way members of a human community do. Each person is a unique individual and has his or her own talents and strengths. When two or more people come together, they combine their efforts by using their own strengths. One person may be good at writing music but not so good at singing. She will then find a person to sing her songs, and together the two of them will be able to form a musical group that many people can appreciate. Independently, neither of them may have ever accomplished anything musically.

Now that you have loaded individual runes, you can load them into groups. Simply write or carve the series of runes you want to use onto a strip of wood or parchment paper. Combined, the individual runes will now take on a modified purpose. Runic energies can be combined using a very ancient technique that results in bind runes, and these can be found on many different carvings. Bind runes work by combining the energy of two or more runes to make one new energy form. This new energy is a singular energy, but it is now something that is beyond the definitions in the Futhark.

Bind runes look like individual runes stacked on top of each other. This example shows Fehu (ᚠ) and Uruz (ᚢ) as a bind rune.

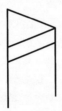

The bind rune Fehu (ᚠ) and Uruz (ᚢ)

From the ancient carvings come special bind runes composed of Mannaz (ᛗ) and Ehwaz (ᛖ); this bind rune means a man riding on a horse. Today, it could represent a person riding in a car.

The bind rune Mannaz (ᛗ) and Ehwaz (ᛖ)

Another special bind rune is the word *alu*, shown below. The only visible runes are Ansuz (ᚠ) and Uruz (ᚢ). Laguz (ᛚ) is stacked on top of Ansuz.

The bind rune alu, composed of Ansuz (ᚠ), Uruz (ᚢ), and Laguz (ᛚ)

A good practice for learning about the look of bind runes is to write out your name. First, write your name in runes as normal. Then practice different methods of stacking the runes until you find one that is aesthetically pleasing. Now you have a magical representation of your name that you can use on future workings. It may be interesting to take the time and analyze the runes of your name to see what the runic energy is like. Here are two examples:

Runes of the name *Bill* as a bind rune, left; and runes of the name *Brenda* as a bind rune, right

Working with bind runes is very similar to writing a sentence. In a sentence, there is always a subject. The subject rune would be the primary rune that is to be modified. In the sentence, you will have a verb, and you may have adjectives. In a bind rune, these are the parts that describe how you want the subject runic energy to be modified.

For example, let's examine figure 1, the combination of Fehu and Uruz. If Fehu were the subject, we could be working with a money concept. Uruz could bring vitality and strength to this concept. We may even say that this bind rune means "strong money," such as money that could be used for down payments or investments.

Alternatively, if Uruz is the subject, we may be working with health issues. The Fehu would be what is paid into such issues. On the surface, paying into health issues may mean paying a doctor bill. It can also mean something entirely different. Fehu need not always be money; it is simply a medium of exchange. In this case, the energy could be time, effort, and a commitment to improving health. Therefore, Uruz and Fehu combined could be the energy of exercise, eating right, and motivation.

Determining what energy is needed really comes down to the person doing the work and to the need at hand. You can see how easily a bind rune can take on two different meanings. So when working with runes, you must be clear in your intention and set on a direct and focused purpose. Do not let the runic energy stray, or it will find its own way and the results may not be what you intend.

When it comes to the loading of bind runes, you may start by stating the runes' names. Then you may state the few words that best describe your bind runes, such as "strong money" or "motivation to improve health." This phrase will help to focus your conscious mind and guide your subconscious into the feelings that you need.

One of the best uses for bind runes is as inner runes. Once you have determined your strengths or weaknesses, you can use other runes to help modify them. For example, you may be seeking a job interview. You may know that you easily get nervous and have a difficult time speaking in interview situations. This knowledge would indicate that your Ansuz needs a boost. Now you just need to identify what runes will enhance the Ansuz in the direction that you needed.

If you add Uruz to Ansuz, the bind rune you create may speak of bold words and confidence. Thurisaz could give you harsh and attacking means of communication and may not be the best idea for an interview. Another possibility could be Laguz. If you know you understand what it is you want to say, but there is a block in the flow of information from your memory to your mouth, Laguz may provide that flow. Another potential modifier rune could be Jera, which, combined with Ansuz, would be a successful outpouring of words for gaining a goal.

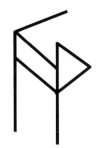

The bind rune Ansuz (ᚠ), Laguz (ᛚ), and Jera
(ᛃ)—"a successful outpouring of words"

Keep in mind that you would need to find only a few words to describe each of these combinations. The combined runes Ansuz (ᚠ) and Uruz (ᚢ) would be "strong words" or "speaking confidently"; Ansuz (ᚠ) and Laguz (ᛚ) would be "easily flowing words"; Ansuz (ᚠ) and Jera (ᛃ) could be "successful communication" or "bountiful outpouring of words." To combine them all, one might find "a confident and easy flowing of words for success." This process of creating bind runes is only limited by your imagination and motivation.

In summary, using the runes you have learned is very powerful and transformative. It is really bound only by your understanding and imagination. There is so much that the runes can do to modify the energy of the many layers of your reality, knowing this is just the first step in understanding the runes' full potential to transform your life. At this point, the work at hand is to experiment. Come up with various ideas of energy that you would like to transform. Then take that energy and apply different runes to it. Start with the conscious mind. Think about what its energy is and how it can be changed. Then check in with your feelings; do your feelings and conscious mind have common ground? If so, go ahead and try to create bind runes. Start small and easy. Remember that the energy shift is only subtle. These runes may set up the process for success, but you must really get up and take action before that success can be realized.

Exercise 5: Bind Rune Analysis

This exercise is not used to create bind runes, but to help you understand how the energies of runes work together to form complementary new energies. You will actively engage your understanding of the runes with your imagination.

The goal of this exercise is twofold: First, you will deepen your understanding of each of the runes and better memorize their properties. Second, you will see just how these energies mingle.

You do not need a loaded set of runes for this process, but it will help. This exercise is actively engaging the imagination that exists in your conscious and subconscious mind. It will also test your memorization skills. If you do have a loaded set of runes, you may find that the subtle energy helps trigger your understanding. As your hold the runes, their runic energy will seep into your being. Some part of you will connect with them. As that part connects, it will communicate the rune's energetic information to your sub-conscious. Your subconscious will then communicate this energetic information to your conscious mind. The information may come as feelings, twitches in the body, sights, sounds, smells, or any other sort of sensory experience. It may simply come as words.

Even if this process does not happen, your conscious mind is aware of the name and function of the runic energy, and your subtle awareness will meet it in the middle, where your conscious and subconscious communicate with each other. This balanced approach will lead you to a deeper level of understanding of the runes.

The Process

You will need your runes that you have created and somewhere to log your observations. If you have been keeping a journal of your rune work, use it here. (See the separate Bind Rune Study Log page.) If not, it will still be beneficial for you to write down your results. You may find that, over time, your understanding of the runes will change and your answers to the same combinations may differ. Looking back will help you to see how you have changed and to identify the underlying energy of the runes. It may even give you a glimpse of your evolution on the subtle levels of reality.

This exercise takes place in a meditative space. Set up an en-vironment that is conducive to this type of working. Candles and incense will help. Invoking a deity and spirits to assist you in clarify-ing your understanding will help. There is not a strong requirement to set up protection for this space, but if you feel the need, then do so. It is best to do this exercise in a sitting position, preferably at a table. You will be handling your runes and will need a place to set them and the paper on which you will write your observations.

A helpful next step is to look through the meanings of the runes one more time. You may want to have your inner runes exercise (exercise 4) and pages describing the runes (chapter 2) bookmarked and available for reference.

Once you are settled in your meditative place, pull two runes out of your bag or box. Write down the runes names and what their individual meanings are. Now think about what these two runes would mean if they were one rune. First, look at the combination directly. Sometimes it helps to take one word for each rune and put them together. For example, the word for Fehu (ᚠ) would be *money*, and the word for Jera (ᛃ) would be *boon*. Together, these two runes could mean "an abundance of money." Now, reverse the words' order and see what that meaning is. In the case of Fehu and Jera, reversing the words could turn the same two runes to mean "the money paid to a successful investment." Log both of these meanings. Keeping your imagination fully engaged, try to metaphorically describe this new meaning. "An abundance of money" may come from an inheritance, a raise or bonus at work, or even a winning lottery ticket. The key here is to find a real-world connection to the words you are describing.

Now engage the feeling of these runes. If both descriptions are true and accurate, what is the underlying energy? This part may or may not have words. If you can find the words, write them down. Either way, take some time sitting with this energy so that you understand it on all levels.

Feel free to continue this process, pulling two runes at a time. Set each pair to the side so that you do not pull them again in your subsequent readings. When you have completed going through all of the runes, stop. You have done enough for one day. Take some time now and go back through your notes to see if you find any sort of pattern. You may be surprised to find that all of the runes may have been working together to describe a bigger picture or situation.

BIND RUNE STUDY LOG

Please feel free to copy this page into your journal. Copy it as many times as needed to cover all of the runes in your practice.

■ Remember to work with only two runes at a time. When you pull two runes, note which one is the subject rune. Then look at how the other rune's energies modify it. Write down this description. Then reverse the runes, so that the second rune is the subject rune and the first is the modifier. Write down a brief meaning of this second combination.

■ Set these runes aside, choose two more runes, and repeat the process.

	Stave	Rune name	One- or two-word description of energy

Rune 1: _____ _____ _____

Rune 2: _____ _____ _____

Description of combined runic energy: _____

_____

_____

Alternate description of combined runic energy: _____

_____

_____

Divination

The following technique of working with the runes is actually a form of runic divination. It is not used to predict the future or tell fortunes. Rather, this process is a diagnostic tool used to tap into your subconscious and see what is going on. The deeper parts of your mind connect you with your body and with your spirit. There may be things your body and soul are trying to tell you, yet you may miss the communication. Sometimes we block out what we most desperately need to know about ourselves. Working with the runes in this way bypasses the prejudices and interpretations of the conscious mind.

For this diagnostic process, pull rune combinations as you did for the first part of exercise 5, but do not limit your pulls to only two runes. Sometimes the phrase that needs to come out is more complex than what two runes can say. Let your hand pull as many runes as seem to fall into it. This may be as few as one and as many as five or more.

Put down the runes you draw face up and upright. There are no negative energies to the runes, so they cannot be read in reverse. Now look to this group of runes. As before, assign one or two words to each rune and put those words together in a phrase; you may actually find a sentence coming forth. You may also need to use your imagination to determine what these runes are describing. They may have presented you with an abstract concept of something they are trying to convey. The advice here is not to judge. Simply record what you are receiving.

Now pull a second set of runes and repeat the process. Continue pulling sets until all runes have been pulled.

If you feel compelled to stop before you've pulled all the runes, follow this notion and put the rest of your runes to the side. Some people have put into their rune collection a piece of wood that is the same shape and size as the other pieces. This piece is blank or has some other, nonrunic character. Its purpose is to notify them to stop pulling runes. It is the stopping stave.

When you have completed pulling the runes, look them over for a complete picture. It may take some analyzing and studying for you to see what they are trying to tell you. More often than not, the resultant reading is told like a story. You will find a problem described and advice for a potential resolution.

With the bind-rune process, you analyzed the various ways the runic combinations could be understood. With this diagnostic process, do not try to come up with alternate meanings for the rune combinations. It is important to take the first impression you are given. This first hint as to the nature of the message is quite often the most accurate.

The only bit of interpretive work that may be needed is to find the real-world reflection. For example, you may know you are dealing with money in abundance, but you need to discern how that money is coming. This could be in the form of a winning lottery ticket, a raise or bonus at work, or any other source of income. The beauty is that some part of you really knows where this boon is coming from. Ask yourself, are you looking for a raise? Are you doing the right things to receive extra income? If not, what is happening in your world that could bring in the extra money? If you are at a loss, the other sets of runes may fill in the gaps.

This diagnostic process is not just limited to the understanding of yourself. We are all connected at the collective-unconscious level of reality. Therefore you can use these runes, in this diagnostic way, to help others understand what is happening to them as well. You first need to obtain their permission to do this working. Then, as you are stirring your runes, before the first pull, move the person's energy into the runes. This movement is simply a state of intention. If you intend to read for this person, then you will. If you feel you would rather have the person put their own energy into the runes by stirring or pulling them themselves, have them do so. How the process unfolds is up to you. All of these methods have worked with great success.

GALDRATHULA-RUNIC MANTRA

Galdr, an Old Norse spiritual system, employed the use of runes. *Galdr* literally means "to sing or utter." This meaning tells us that the best way to use the runes was not to carve and load physical staves, but rather to sing the runes' names. This makes sense, as a thousand years ago stories were passed down not in writing but in spoken verse. A majority of the population was not literate enough to read or carve runes, but they could understand speech. Speech was so important that it was said a man who was of any worth was as good at composing poetry as he was in battle.

The galdr use of runes is perhaps the most important use, as well as the most powerful one. As seen in the previous chapter, intoning the name of the rune can fill a person with the energy of that rune. The reason this works is that a harmonic resonance is set up through various layers of reality.

Runic Vibrations

All energy has a frequency of vibration; runic energy is no different. When a vibration is cast out, everything that resonates with this energy also vibrates to the frequency of this energy. We can think of these corresponding energies like two violins. They both are tuned exactly to the notes of G, D, A, and E. If one violin's G string is played loudly near the other violin, the second violin's G string will vibrate. The same thing happens if the other open strings are played. When a musician puts a finger down on a violin string, the frequency of the note played will change. If a finger is placed on the G string of the first violin, and that violin is now playing A, then the G string on the second violin will not resonate.

This concept is also true of runic energy. As you verbally intone the name of a rune, you set up a vibration of air in the room about you. You also begin to vibrate your body. As your body is vibrating with the sound, your cells and molecules within your body begin to resonate with this vibration as well. You are literally making your body and the room sounding boards for runic energy.

The next step in the process of intoning runes is to turn your thoughts inward. As you do, your mind begins to create a singular focus on the vibration of the tone. When you add conscious thought to the vibration, the change in consciousness makes your subconscious receptive. When you sing a rune and think of its purpose, this energy sinks deeper into your mind, and your subconscious connects with the concepts.

Since the subconscious is not too keen on using words, it has a direct access to the spiritual level of reality, which does not use any sort of physical communication. When your subconscious mind tunes into the specific runic energies you are intoning, it changes the spiritual energy of your being. When that happens, all the levels of your reality begin to resonate with a runic charge. Your subconscious mind merely opens the door for the spiritual level of reality to generate this energy. As your body resonates with the sound of the rune, the rune's energy is brought forth into the objective level of reality, where it can be manifested.

As all of this is happening, you are continuously drawing in a neutral energy from the Ginnic level of reality. This energy has no shape or form. Your very breath becomes the focusing vehicle to draw in this energy. As this neutral energy hits the vibrations you are making, it instantly changes to match the vibration. You now have an abundance of energy, charged to a particular runic energy, that can be used for whatever your intention is.

When you have an abundance of energy and all of your being is tuned to this energy, something very interesting starts to happen.

You begin to alter your reality at a very subtle level. Here is how it works: The cells of your body are made up of molecules. All of these molecules vibrate at a certain frequency. Since they came from a universal point of creation, they have the potential to vibrate at any frequency. We all have a Ginnic origin, and all of the runes currently exist within us. We are susceptible, at the molecular level, to these runic vibrations. As our molecules and cells vibrate to a new frequency, they begin to change. They become tuned to a new way of being. This process will also cause your cells to purge chemicals that are not conducive to your new way of being. They will begin searching for the new chemicals of your new existence. Every emotion has a chemical, and the chemicals your cells will accept will change with this process. The cells that once were used for disappointment or rejection will now readily accept the chemicals of satisfaction and happiness. Since similarities attract and perpetuate, you will easily be drawn into situations that suit your new way of being and that are beneficial to your goals.

This effect from the energy shift can be locked into place by the repetition of the runes. As you state the name of the rune you are using over and over, your subconscious becomes programmed with its energies. Your subconscious now has a belief set in place that this runic concept is the only reality there is. As this energy is continuing to vibrate your molecules and spiritual energy, those too become programmed with the runic energy. The more you intone a rune and draw its energy in, the more your entire reality becomes altered to match the runic energy. Even when you are done, there are trace levels of this energy. It takes awhile for the realities to return to their home state. When this process is repeated many times, the runic vibrations may actually become your realities' new home state.

At this point the power of words comes into play. The English language originates from the languages that used runes. Many of the words we speak today have a direct link to the same runic energies that were alive a thousand or more years ago, and these words have specific runic vibrations tied to them. Think of it—even when you say the word *fee*, you have a conscious awareness of the meaning of the word and a feeling of what the word means. As you say the word *fee*, you are tuning your entire being to that word and to the energy of Fehu.

This vibrational connection is why it is so critical that you become aware of the words you use. Your reality, at all levels, stems from the very words you use every day. Your words are a reflection of the state of mind you are in. With them, your state of mind sets up a spiritual connection. As you learned in the loading exercise, every breath you take fills you with a neutral universal energy, and energy that is tuned with your intentions is cast out into the world with your words. Therefore, every word you speak, be it in jest, as a compliment, or with contempt, sets up a harmonic resonance that tunes your entire reality to that word.

The more you say that word, the more your subconscious becomes engrained with it. Your subconscious now believes that this view is the one and only way that reality can exist. You become your words; your daily language becomes your reality. By reading this book and understanding these concepts, you are ready to embark on a process that will literally change your reality.

The ancient spiritual leaders who sang the runes tapped into the runic energies and passed their ideas of the runes on through the ages. Their rune work was done in the spiritual and Ginnic levels of reality. On these levels, there is no such thing as time or space. All of spiritual reality happens at once, and all things are connected there. This connection means that as you sing the runes today, you tap into the same energy that was used over a thousand years ago. This connection creates a temporal resonance, in addition to the harmonic resonance that you create through your entire being when you sing the runes.

Becoming part of this temporal harmonic resonance has many benefits. First, it connects you with the ancient people who used these runes. As you draw this runic energy to you, it becomes your home state, little by little. As it does, you will draw ancient rune masters to you. They will become teachers whispering ancient wisdom into your being and helping you to improve your world. Another benefit to joining with the temporal harmonic resonance is it adds strength, purpose, and authenticity to your work. When you sing the same words and sounds that were sung over a thousand years ago, you are participating in a tried-and-true system of transformation. Runes have helped thousands of people over the eons achieve their goals, and they can help you too.

This process of tuning into temporal harmonic resonance is similar to what is known as complementary waves. As waves of the same frequency encounter each other, their energy is increased (see the individual runic vibrations below). You can think of this encounter as like having two radios tuned to the same station. The radios' combined sounds are louder than those of the individual radios by themselves. As you tap into runic energy, you are combining the vibrations of the air, your body, your spirit, and the temporal harmonic resonance into a massive waveform (see the combined energies below). This waveform will penetrate through all of time and levels of reality, causing the subtle shifts you seek to make.

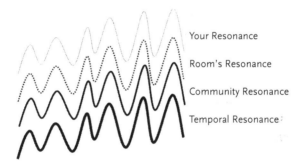

Your Resonance

Room's Resonance

Community Resonance

Temporal Resonance

The individual runic vibrations meet and combine.

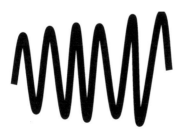

A new, massive runic waveform is created with the combined resonating energies.

Runic Power Words

Of the multitude of objects carved with runes, there are only a few that can be specifically pointed to as being magical tools. These amulets are called bracteates. They have intricate knotwork, patterns, beasts, and sometimes faces carved on them. Also on these bracteates are rune charms. Sometimes these charms are sentences; sometimes they are just a single word or even a single rune or two. These amulets helped the wearers with various situations they faced.

To strengthen the charms, there were a few common words. These words may still be used today, even though they are in an ancient tongue. As you understand the intention of the words, the vibrations of the words, just like the runes that make up those words, still carry the potential for temporal resonance. What follows is a list of these words, their meanings, and use.

Laukaz (ᛚᛅᚢᚲᛅᛉ)

Laukaz (*lau-KAHZ*, with an "au" sound like the "*ou*" in house or mouse) is one of the most commonly repeated words found on amulets. Its origin may be related to that of the words for the family of plants that includes leeks, onions, and garlic. Norse folk wisdom said that putting a leek in beer protected the drinker against poison. Leeks were also used for many different types of healing works, tying *laukaz* to healing, antidotes, and medicine. Used on an amulet or in galdring, *laukaz* brings healing energy to a person.

Lathu (ᛚᛅᚦᚢ)

The word *lathu* (*LA-thoo*) is a formal and polite invitation. Its main purpose seems to have been the invocation of a deity and the summoning of spiritual forces. There is some evidence suggesting that, as language evolved, *lathu* was connected with the word *load*. We can think of *lathu* as a way to call spiritual and divine energies to us and then to charge, or load, a person or object with that energy.

An example of a runic formula using *lathu* is found on the Borringe bracteate, an amulet from fifth-century Sweden:

lathu laukaz
inviting healing

These words invoke and load healing energy. The Borringe bracteate may have been one worn by a healer to allow healing energy to flow through him or her.

Another example of how *lathu* was used is from the Darum bracteate, an amulet from fifth-century Denmark, which reads *Frohila Lathu. Frohila* is a name used for Freyr, the deity of male fertility and a giver of wealth. This bracteate may have been used to empower its wearer with virility and wealth.

Auja (ᚠᚢᚲᚠ)

Auja (*AU-ya*, with an "*au*" sound like the "*ou*" in house or mouse) has a couple of possible definitions. It is most commonly taken to mean luck; it could also be taken as divine protection. Often, *auja* follows the word *gibu*, which is etymologically connected to *Gebo*. This connection shows that *gibu* represents generosity or the giving of gifts. *Gibu auja*, then, would be the giving of luck or protection.

We see this phrase on the Seeland-II-C bracteate, an amulet found in Zealand, Denmark, dating to the fifth century:

hariuha haitaka farauisa gibo auja ᛏᛏᛏ
hariuha, I am called, dangerous, giver of luck, ᛏᛏᛏ

The three Tiwaz runes would be the direct invocation of the energy of that rune. As Tiwaz was often carved on weapons to protect the warriors in battle, this *gibo auja* formula may be one that gives the wearer luck and protection in combat.

Uiki (ᚢᚲᛁ, ᚢᛁᚲᛁ)

This word shows up on the occasional bracteate. It is more commonly found on rune stones that use a later form of the runic alphabet, one that has fewer rune staves. (The Younger Futhark would pair up phonetic values with a single stave. For example, the stave of Ur (Uruz) serves double duty: it has value of *u* and *v*. The stave of Kaun (Kennaz) is both *k* and *g*.) There is no clear indication of how *uiki* is to be pronounced. Some will say it sounds like *vigi* or *viki*; others will pronounce it *uiki*. Whatever the pronunciation, its meaning is agreed upon: it means to bless and protect.

We see this word on the Velanda Stone, a rune stone raised in tenth-century Sweden:

> *Thur uiki thasi runar*
> Thor protect/bless these runes

This phrase is repeated on other stones, to protect the runes or even the monument itself.

Used as a runic formula, *uiki* would bring the energy of protection and blessing to a person, object, or the runes carved. It is often connected with Thor, as he is the god who is known to protect the other gods and mankind. While *uiki* is not historically known to be used in connection with any other deity or used alone as a blessing formula, it could be. Use it as you feel appropriate, as no ill effect can come from its use.

Alu (ᚨᛚᚢ)

Modern researchers debate the origin and meaning of *alu*. Some will argue that its origin is tied with the root of the word *ale*. Some suggest that it is term that simply means "magic." All will agree that there is some sort of mystical connection with this word.

It often appeared at the end of a runic statement, such as this one from the Funen bracteate, an amulet from fifth-century Denmark:

> *Lathu aaduaaaliia Alu*
> Invocation "magical phrase" manifest

Lathu is "invocation." *Aaduaaaliia* is a rune formula that only the rune master may know the meaning of; one can only speculate about the intention of the unreadable rune script. *Alu* ends the phrase in order to manifest this formula's energy into reality.

On the Skrystrup bracteate, yet another amulet dating back to fifth-century Denmark, appears as:

Laukaz Alu
Healing magic

This phrase is the calling of healing power. On many other bracteates and stones *alu* appears alone.

The best that can be discerned about the meaning of *alu* is that it has the power of manifestation; that is, *alu* is used to help bring intentions into reality. We have seen how this works with the alu formula (see chapter 5). We know that runes are living beings that each have a singular focus. When combined, their energies complement each other. When runes or rune words are combined with *alu*, the singular purpose of the combined phrase is the manifestation of the chosen runes' energy.

The Hindu and Tibetan traditions have a similar word, *aum* or *om*, which may or may not be connected to *alu*. *Aum* comes at the start of a mantra. It awakens the third-eye chakra and helps to bring about the mantra that follows it. *Alu* does the same thing, only it comes at the end of the runic mantra.

Connected to *aum*, at least by sound, is the English phrase "I am." These two words are powerfully transformative. They have a very similar vibrational energy to *aum* and *alu*, and they cause the conscious and subconscious mind to believe what is said with them.

When a person says "I am," what follows the phrase is brought through his or her entire being and into reality. This is a dramatic example of how words change reality.

When people say, "I am sick," "I am dead tired," or "I am sad," they may be truly in that state of being at that moment. But as they repeat these phrases over and over, they program themselves to be in that state. Their mind, in the subconscious and conscious levels, begins to believe the energy of the phrase is the only energy of reality. Then the body becomes programmed to only accept these types of chemicals.

The same is true for those who say, "I am recovering well," "I am happy," or "I keep doing better every day." These people are programming themselves to be in a happier, healthier state.

Since "I am" has a vibrational connection to *alu* and *aum*, they are programming their entire being to be within this state of recovery or success. Be aware of the words you use and how they may be creating your reality.

Deities and the Runes

Other words that may be used with runic formulae are the names of the gods of Norse lore. While you may not be a follower of the Norse spiritual path, the legends of the Norse gods will still serve as a benefit. You may not need to see these deities as gods ruling over the various parts of reality; they can also be seen as archetypes. The legends of the gods can represent the ideal state of being that a person can reach in the same way Buddha is perceived by Buddhists.

In Buddhism, Buddha is not a god. Rather, he represents the ideal state of a human being. Some Buddhists believe that as people progress through lifetimes, they lose the illusion that they are not connected to all things. As soon as they loose this illusion, they become a Buddha themselves. Therefore everyone is a Buddha-to-be as they have this potential within them. Here is a similar concept for you to ponder: just as all humans have the potential to become Buddha, so too do they have the runic potential from the Ginnic source.

This idealization concept is true of the Norse deities as well. The difference is that this potential not only resides within each individual, but within the world around us as well. These gods and goddesses, like the runes, can be found hiding within all things. They are the latent potential energy that can be manifest only when it is tapped into. One must actively seek and engage the gods of the Norse lore for their influence and wisdom to be realized.

When using a deity for runic work, look to the stories to find what his or her functions are. Deities cannot be summed up simply with phrases such as the "god of war" or "goddess of love." Each of them, like people, is a complex being who takes time and openness to fully understand. If you were to take any of the Nordic gods at face value, you may be surprised when you find the complexity of their character below the surface.

Odin

Keywords: communication, wisdom, magic, ecstasy

Odin was the chieftain of gods. He was one of three who created the physical world and humanity. Therefore, he was called Alfather, or the father of all things.

After this creation process, he took on three trials to fully ascend to godhood. He drank from the well of Mimir to learn the fates of all things, he won the mead of poetry and inspiration known as Odhroerir, and he hung upon the world tree for nine nights to gain the power of the runes. For this final task, he was known as Galdrafather, or the father of rune magic.

He was also the ruler of Valhalla, the hall where great warriors ascended to after they were killed in battle. There, they trained to fight in the final battle known as Ragnarok. As ruler of Valhalla, Odin was known as Valfather, or father of the chosen slain.

In ancient days, he was called on for many different types of help, and he meant different things to different people. He was called on by kings and leaders for victory in battle. His advice was paramount to those looking to enhance their leadership skills. The poets and berserkers, warriors known for becoming wild in battle, both called on him. He controlled the bonds that set the berserkers free in battle and enabled the poet to compose easily. Conversely, he could cause writer's block or make a warrior freeze in combat. Odin's wisdom was valued highly. He could see over all of the nine worlds and knows all things. For magic and rune work, Odin was the wisest of all beings.

As we see, Odin is a very complex and almost contradictory deity. It is thought that his name means "ruler of ecstasy." This is the ecstasy and inspiration of warriors, poets, magic workers, and healers. He will help with wisdom, communication, and magic. If you need to work with binding and unbinding, these actions are his territory. Odin's influence is most strongly felt in the Ansuz rune.

Tyr

Keywords: discipline, order, temperance, justice

We have already explored the legend Tyr with the rune Tiwaz (see chapter 2). Tyr was called upon as the god of warriors. Odin granted victory to kings and leaders; Tyr offered protection, temperance, and discipline to the warriors. Quite often, he was invoked with a simple carving of the Tiwaz rune. On amulets and weapons, Tiwaz can be found carved in groups of three. This is seen on the Seeland-II Bracteate. After *"gebo auja,"* ↑↑↑ was carved. Sometimes a sole Tiwaz stave was carved upon a sword to call upon his gifts.

Today, we benefit from everything Tyr has to offer. Many of us may not be warriors, but we may need help with his sense of discipline, structure, and order. We also may call upon him for victory in cases where we are due justice. It must be noted that this call must be for the right, true, and noble cause. Tyr will always side with noble and just causes. Tyr's energy will also bring us focus and clarity. In matters of the mind, the Tiwaz energy can help one's mind stay on track and on one topic at a time.

Thor

Keywords: protection, blessings, powerful and dynamic energy

Thor was the protector of the people. Therefore, he was awarded the title Folk Warder. The image of his hammer was, and is, worn by people as a reminder of his protection. Thor and his hammer were called upon for blessings, as well as protection. A blessed hammer was placed in the lap of a bride to ensure fertility and protect the family line. The hammer was used to clear energies and to protect homes and hallowed spaces. It was even used for blessings in a funeral. Thor's energy blessed and protected everything and everyone from before birth to after death.

We may call upon Thor's energy for this protection. His energy is active and powerful. When this energy is called upon, seldom is there calm. Thor may also be called upon for the blessing and protection of anything that is in need. It is quite common to call upon him with the words *Thor Vigi* or even *Lathu Thor*.

Freyr

Keywords: male fertility, wealth, prosperity, peace

Freyr is the patron deity of Sweden. The royal lineage of long ago claimed they were descended from the line of Ingvar Freyr. Freyr was a member of the fertility and nature deities called the Vanir. Therefore, he is seen as the ruler of the natural world. It is his seed that helps all things grow, including crops, livestock, and families. From this influence, he was also said to control wealth.

Weapons were banned at the worship of Freyr. However, he was symbolized by a vicious golden boar that he rode upon, called Gullenbursti. For this reason, we can assume that Freyr may be a virulent defender of peace.

Freyr is the best of all producers, and he can be called upon today to help boost anything in need of growing. This could be family, plants, or even investments. Freyr is also called upon for peace and friendship. Freyr's influence is found in the rune Inguz.

Freya

Keywords: female fertility, love, beauty, lust

Freya was renowned for her beauty and love. She was the most beautiful and desired of all of the goddesses. She was the twin sister of Freyr and a member of the Vanir. She can be seen as the ruler of female fertility. She was also the granter of beauty and beautiful things. In the ancient days, anything having to do with the beauty of women was Freya's domain. Like her brother, she had a battle-oriented side. It is said she got half of the men slain in battle for her hall, Folkvangr. The warriors in Valhalla train to fight, but there is no fighting in Folkvangr. As Freya was a goddess of lust, Folkvangr may be a hall for the eternal fulfillment of carnal desires.

Today, Freya's energy can still be called upon for many matters. As she oversees all love affairs, her energy will help to raise or rekindle romance. She can help boost libido. If you are in need of advice about beauty, she is the one to go to. Freya's energy will help with matters of fertility and the female reproductive system. Since her energy is that of the fertile field, calling upon her energy may bring about fertility in any way you need it, but only if you have a seed that needs to be planted in that field. When you work with the Berkana rune, you are working with the fertile energies of Freya.

Frigga

Keywords: home and hearth, family, nurturing

Not too much is known about Frigga. She was the wife of Odin and the only deity who can best him in a battle of wits. It is said she knew the fates of all things, yet said nothing. She was symbolized by linen, the flax plant, and spindle whorls. Spinning textiles was a common chore for women a thousand years ago. Therefore, Frigga's mysteries can be unraveled with the magic of weaving and spinning.

Frigga's energy will help with any issue having to do with the home or family. She may be called upon to end strife within a home or even to help you find a home. The energy of Frigga is a perfect complement to that of Freya. Where Freya represents the action of reproduction, Frigga is the care and nurturing of the family. She can help with all aspects of family, ranging from help with the spouse to help with the children.

Eir

Keywords: health, healing

Frigga had twelve handmaidens, each with her own function. One of them was Eir. It is said that Eir was the foremost of all physicians. She was called upon for any type of healing or health concern. Today, the simple runic phrase *Eir lathu gebo laukaz* will call her and bring her healing energy to a person.

Forseti

Keywords: balance, mediation, legal issues

Forseti is the son of Baldr, the most loved of all the gods. The legend of Forseti shows him teaching fair and equitable laws to a council of twelve lawmakers. He was able to speak to all of them so that they understood his teachings and could agree upon a common ground. For this reason, Forseti was called upon to quell any sort of legal issue. He is the best of all mediators. He can help both sides come to an agreement. There is no one rune that sums up Forseti's energy. However, combining Tiwaz (↑) with Gebo (✕), Mannaz (ᛗ), and/or Wunjo (ᚹ) will bring about the balance and order that is sacred to Forseti.

Runes and Affirmations

Today, we have a powerful tool for transformations that fits perfectly with the ancient practice of Galdr. This tool also uses words and is highly effective for retraining your mind. It is called the affirmation.

Affirmations are effectively used in a wide variety of fields. Businesspeople use them to get themselves ready for sales or to overcome challenges. Athletes use affirmations to boost and enhance performance. Performers use affirmations to quell anxiety and focus their minds before a performance. Affirmations are even used to help encourage a person to heal, control pain, or overcome addiction.

How Affirmations Work

We have seen the power of words and runic phrases to alter reality on all levels. Affirmations do the same thing. They come from the science of psychology and are best described using the theory that developed them. Affirmations primarily affect you on two levels, the conscious and subconscious. Quite often, affirmations are written at the secular level. If you choose to include any sort of spiritual or religious reference in your affirmation, then it will affect you on the spiritual level as well.

Initially, an affirmation brings the intended goal to the awareness of the conscious mind. You state your chosen phrase several times, often a few times a day. This repetition trains the conscious mind to adopt the thinking and use of the words in the affirmation. The affirmation serves as a constant reminder of what you are working on. Because you repeat your affirmation or keep it posted near you, you never stray from your goal. You are constantly aware of your goal and how you are achieving it.

If you do an action repetitively, you are naturally inclined to move into a slight trance state. In this trance state, your level of suggestibility is increased. When you repeat an affirmation, you are brought into this trancelike state. In this state, your subconscious mind latches on to the meaning and concept of the affirmation. It begins to believe that this affirmation is indeed reality. This process is cumulative. The more times the affirmation process is repeated, the deeper this belief becomes ingrained. The deeper parts of your psyche are now programmed with the belief that your goal is achievable.

When the conscious and subconscious are brought into alignment, the physical reality of the affirmation is easier to bring about. You will find your task easy to perform, and you will like doing it. What once was an unsuccessful chore is now a light at the end of a very short tunnel.

There are a few secrets to making the affirmation successful. The first is to understand that the mind is like a muscle. The more it is used, the stronger it gets. If a muscle is used too much or improperly, it becomes fatigued or even damaged. Affirmations work in this way as well; they are the heavy lifting of the mind.

If you recite your mantra too often, your mind will rebel against it. For this reason, you need to take a rest from reciting your affirmation. This rest allows the brain to rebuild its neural pathways. As it does, the subconscious is very active, applying this new message to situations it is familiar with. As this affirmation becomes deeply ingrained, the subconscious mind uses it as a template against which future situations are measured. Your once-insurmountable obstacle will, without your knowing it, become a challenge that is easily met.

The best way to use an affirmation is to repeat it ten times, then stop. Repeat this process three times a day. You can also write down the affirmation and carry it in a pocket or purse. Some people hang it on the door so they see it before they leave their house. Dieters post affirmations on their refrigerators. People working to achieve their goals at work post it near their desks. Reading the posted affirmation will remind the conscious and subconscious mind about the work at hand.

To be truly powerful, the affirmation needs to be stated, posted, and kept in the mind for a brief moment in time, then released. As it is released, the real work begins. The undercurrents of the mind are being rewired and programmed for success.

It is recommended that you follow the affirmation process for at least twenty-one days. When something is done for twenty-one to twenty-seven days, it becomes a habit. When you reach the twenty-one-day point with an affirmation, thinking it becomes a habit for the mind.

This wisdom works with the Hindu mantra as well. They say to do the mantra process for twenty-seven days. (Twenty-seven is a sacred number, tied to the number nine, which is sacred to the Norse traditions as well.) It is said that as one nears the twenty-seventh day of repeating the mantra, he or she may feel ill or out of sorts. This illness may be the body or soul clearing away negative energy. It may also be the part of the person that is unwilling to change. It is literally fighting back. The advice is to hold steady. Upon completing twenty-seven days of the mantra, the person will return to health and good spirits.

This same phenomenon happens with affirmations. You may encounter a period of inner rebellion. This is common and should be expected. When encountering this resistance, it is best to be gentle and understanding with yourself. Keep up the process, and this resistance should resolve. If it does not, it might be an indication that there is something deeper involved. You can then try a different affirmation or seek outside help.

Another secret to making affirmations work is the rule of the three p's. Keep the affirmation in the *present tense*, *positive*, and *possible*. Keeping an affirmation in line with these three concepts makes it acceptable to the subconscious and helps to avoid inner resistance.

We have all encountered situations where we said one thing yet intended another. This same thing happens when we put together phrases for ourselves to follow and believe. Sometimes we say one thing but intend another, and in order to get to the true message, we must read between the lines. The subconscious cannot read between the lines. For information from the conscious mind to be easily accepted, it needs to be stated directly and clearly. The subconscious will not be able to filter out an implied message; it can't take a hint. For this reason, composing an affirmation using the rule of three *p*'s will help to make the message direct and easily digestible to the subconscious mind.

Present

Keywords: now, today, every day, every time

It is important to keep the phrase in the present tense. The subconscious mind has no concept of time or place. For this part of your mind, everything that ever happened is still happening. It has no sense of past, present, or future. Everything is in the here-and-now.

When you want to implant a message into the subconscious, you must state it as if it is currently happening. For instance, "I am in the process of _____" or "I am becoming healthier each day."

Positive

Keywords: achieving, accomplishing, becoming, moving toward

The subconscious mind does not respond to negative statements. If the statement sent to the subconscious is "I am no longer eating too much," it does not pick up on the negative part of the statement. But there is a risk that it will pick up on the rest of the statement and be programmed to eat too much.

Plus, when a statement is kept positive, it keeps the conscious mind aware of a goal. Your actual goal may not be to stop eating too much, but to improve your health and lose weight. In that case, a positive statement would be, "I am eating healthily to lower my cholesterol, improve my health, and lose weight."

Possible

Keywords: little by little, in a healthy way, easily, step by step

If the dream is too outlandish or the goal too big, the subconscious mind will not even recognize it. The ego will come into play and reject the notion being presented. If you truly are looking to accomplish a large goal, break it down into smaller pieces.

For example, if you were looking to start a business, actually having and running the business may be a huge step. You would need to break it down. Statements such as, "I am now building capital to start my business" or "I am laying a foundation for a successful business" are acceptable to the subconscious mind.

• • •

A key term that may help you form an effective affirmation is *becoming*. If you know your goal lies in the future and the steps you take now will lead you to that goal, you can use *becoming*. Statements like "I am becoming financially independent" or "I am losing weight" will work, but they are not specific in their execution. If you find an affirmation to be unclear or you have a hard time coming up with the specifics, it is OK to start with one vague statement. What you will find is that your mind will open up to the possibility of your success. When that happens, the specific steps to achieving that success will reveal themselves more easily.

The final piece that helps an affirmation to work is the phrase "I am." This phrase connects with the energies of *aum* and *alu* and manifests your affirmation into reality. In addition, it places you into the affirmation. Without this personal connection, there is no self-transformation.

Using the Futharks with Affirmations

Affirmations are ideal places to put into effect everything you have learned about runes so far. For the most part, you are free to add runes, bind runes, runic words, and the names of deities to your statement as you wish. There is only one additional rule: add *alu* to the end of the statement. *Alu* makes the statement effective and gives it the power of manifestation. It will make the statement a powerful runic affirmation, or runic mantra, which is called a *Galdrathula*.

The word *Galdrathula* is made up of two words. The first is *galdr*, the word used for spoken rune magic. The second is *thula*. In the Norse and Germanic traditions, there were sacred speakers or singers called Thule. They were the leaders of religious ceremonies. The songs they sang were like mantras and called *thula*, a word that may mean "lay" or "story," as in "the Lay of Rig." It could also mean "recitation," "rhapsody," "song," or even "mantra." Therefore, a Galdrathula is a magical runic mantra or rune song.

To use a Galdrathula, first come up with a workable affirmation. Then add in the appropriate runes and/or words to it. Refer back to your list of inner-rune definitions. Then you can pick what words will fit. Your Galdrathula will work directly on those parts of your being indicated by the inner runes. If an affirmation sticks with just the words, it will affect only the conscious and subconscious. When you add a spiritual element of an inner rune to it, it now will affect your entire being and make it deeply personal, enhancing the effect profoundly.

Here are some examples of successful Galdrathula:

I am getting healthier each and every day.
(*Lathu Eir, gebo laukaz, alu.*)

Quickly, easily, and healthily, I am losing weight every day.
(*Uruz Jera, alu.*)

I am laying the foundation for a successful business.
(*Hail Freyr, gebo auja.*)

Every day, I am nearing completion of my degree.
(*Fehu Kennaz Jera, alu.*)

I am prepared and fully ready to win my court case.
(*Tiwaz Fehu Laguz, Tyr lathu, Forseti lathu*
gebo auja "victory," alu.)

There are various tools and techniques that will help you remember and use your Galdrathula. Malas, or small beaded necklaces, can be purchased for a reasonable price. They are available with different stones. The stones in these malas have different types of energy.

Writing down the Galdrathula is a very common way to help you remember it. Just like an affirmation, it can be posted anywhere that it will be visible. Some people will place it in their wallet. That way, every time they open it, they are reminded of their workings. It can be burned in a candle flame for energetic results. It can be placed in a stream, and the moving waters will allow the runes to take effect. Some may choose to bury it so that the earth energies can allow the runic energies to grow.

Galdrathulas can also be loaded into carved runes. Rune staves should be carved specifically for use with the Galdrathula. When you carve them, you must keep the intention of your working in mind. You may choose to carve the staves into individual pieces of wood or put all of the individual runes, bind runes, and runic words (written in the form of staves) onto one piece of wood. Some people have used wood stains, paint, or wood burning to put their runes onto wood when carving them was not possible. Load each stave or bind-rune shape individually with its specific energy. Then do a complete loading, saying the full Galdrathula out loud.

Individual carved staves may be kept in a bag and carried. If the runes are carved into one piece of wood, you may keep the piece of wood in a sacred place or carry it with you, provided it is small enough. Some choose to bury it, cover it in cloth, or hide it in a safe place. Let yourself be compelled as to what to do with this carving.

There is a strong advantage carving out the Galdrathula. Carving it fits very appropriately with the ancient runic techniques. Plus, it brings the runes to full life, so that this runic energy can be brought into reality. It will be as if you had a being fully focused on bringing your new state of reality into existence.

Please bear in mind that no matter what method you choose to convey your Galdrathula, you must still do the work necessary in the real world. If you do not do your part, everything that you have done with the runes will be in vain. These runes are altering your being and your reality so that the reality of your dream may come about. If you do nothing else to realize your goal, it will never happen. You must do your part, and the runes will do theirs.

Exercise 6: Creating Your Galdrathula

The following exercise will guide you through the various stages in setting up a working Galdrathula. It is set up like a survey. The results are only for you to read, so do not hesitate to be fully honest with yourself and your answers.

Be aware that not every step needs to be taken in this process. If you feel you need to leave a step out, then do so. If you feel you need to add more in, do so as well. It is best to keep the Galdrathula simple and direct. For that reason, use caution when adding something to this process.

If you find you are trying to accomplish too much, break it into two Galdrathula. It is OK to be working with up to two at one time. One mantra can help lay a foundation. It would point to the overall goal. Within this framework you may be working on a piece of that goal. This piece would make up a second Galdrathula. As you work from this piece to the next, you may choose to keep the first, overall Galdrathula and change out different sub-Galdrathula as you work through the steps to achieve your goal. For example:

Overall Galdrathula:

> "I am starting a successful lawn-care business"
> (*Fehu Wunjo Jera Freyr lathu gebo auja alu*).

Sub-Galdrathula:

> "I am quickly and easily raising capital to start my business"
> (*Kennaz Sowilo Fehu Jera alu*).

The above Galdrathula examples work well for outer workings. What do we do about inner workings? These can be a bit trickier. The results may not be as clear, and we may trigger things we are not ready to deal with. For this reason, if it is a major issue, it is recommended that you work with a trained professional. These techniques will still work, but there may be underlying issues that need to be understood and dealt with.

Still, Galdrathula are ideal for working with your inner runes. You may choose one or more of your inner runes to work with. Your overall goal would be to modify the inner rune to be in a state that you want.

Let's use the example above of the person starting a lawn-care business. Perhaps he is not quite able to raise the capital he needs. Instead of giving up, he takes some time to reflect on his situation. He takes his runes and does a little inner diagnostic work. He finds that he is having difficulty with speaking and meeting others to help him raise capital.

This issue is in the realm of his inner Fehu (ᚠ). He needs to find a way to boost it so he can speak confidently about the future of the business. To boost his Fehu, he needs a clear picture of his goals, what he needs to achieve them, and what he has to offer to achieve them.

He finds other runes to help modify his inner Fehu: Elhaz and Tiwaz for clarity of mind. These two may be combined into one bind rune for an augmented energetic effect. He also chooses Laguz to help with the flow of his words and conveyance of his dreams. This makes his new Galdrathula:

> "I find it easy to speak to people who wish to
> successfully invest in my lawn-care business"
> (*Fehu Elhaz-Tiwaz Laguz alu*).

Before you create a working Galdrathula, it is a good idea to consult with your runes. Do the divination process found in chapter 5 to gain an understanding of what you face and how to overcome the upcoming challenges. It might be a good idea for you to have the following "My Galdrathula" page copied and ready to write on as you consult your runes. Your answers will give you insight into what your true goals may be.

Sometimes the runes may point you to a goal that may be different than your intention. They are not purposefully misleading you or throwing you off the trail. Remember, a higher part of you is communicating through the runes. You are simply being told there is another goal that you must accomplished first. This goal falls into the area of unfinished business. Once you Karma is clear, your road to success will be unhindered.

MY GALDRATHULA

Affirmation

What is your overall goal? _____

List some steps needed to achieve this goal: _____

_____

_____

Is there a time frame that this goal is to be achieved in? _____

Use the above information to write an affirmation in English. You may want to write out different variations on a scrap piece of paper before writing your final one here. If you need to, make an affirmation for the overall goal and sub-affirmations to be cycled through as you achieve various steps. Remember:

- The phrase "I am" must be someplace in the affirmation.

- Phrase the affirmation in the *present tense*.

- Keep the statement *positive*.

- Make sure the affirmation is something that is *possible*.

Your affirmation: _____

_____

_____

Primary Runes

Look at your affirmation as written in English. What are some runes that apply to its concepts? Write down the names of those runes and one or two words that best describe them. If you are also working with a sub-Galdrathula, look at the first step toward achieving your overall goal. What are some runes that apply to this step, and what words describe each of those runes?

Rune   One- or two-word description

_____   _____

_____   _____

_____   _____

_____   _____

Modifier Runes

Are there any other runes that could be used as modifiers (such as Uruz (ᚢ) for fortifying an aspect, or Laguz (ᛚ) to enable flow)?

Rune   One- or two-word description

_____   _____

_____   _____

_____   _____

_____   _____

Additional Pieces

Are there any runic words that will help this goal become a reality? List the words and their meanings. (You may choose the English versions of these words for your final statement.)

Word   Meaning

_____   _____

_____   _____

_____   _____

Will the energy of a deity help in this situation? Which one(s) and how?

Deity   How his or her energy is used (one or two words)

_____   _____

_____   _____

_____   _____

Putting It All Together

Take your main affirmation and amend it with the additional runic pieces. You may find that an English translation of the runic pieces fits in perfectly with the affirmation part. If so, the English is a perfect integration of the runic pieces.

Don't forget: *alu* ends the Galdrathula.

Write your Galdrathula here. Be willing to try multiple variations. One may suit you better than others. Try different variations of runes and runic words.

_____

_____

_____

_____

_____

ADDITIONAL RUNIC TECHNIQUES

You have now learned various working aspects of the runes. You have learned where the runes come from and how they exist in the world around you. Hopefully, you have come to understand the runes as they exist within you. With this knowledge, you have also picked up a few techniques for using the runes. Now I would like to offer some additional techniques for effectively applying the runes. (This book cannot include all of the techniques of rune work. As you use runes more often and become comfortable with them, you will learn more new, effective ways to use them.)

Using Outer Runes

As you have found, the outer runes exist in all things, and you have experienced identifying the various runic traits in inanimate objects. All you have to do is access that runic energy so you can enhance it for your own use. When using outer runes, you will find exercise 3, "The Futhark in All Things," helpful for identifying the runic traits of inanimate objects. No doubt there are a multitude of objects that you use in your daily life. Each of these objects serves a purpose. If you have an object that you are intimately connected with and you know you will be using it for a long time, it will be a good idea to understand its runic nature. To do this, go back to exercise 3. Go through each of the steps for this object.

Here are some important objects you may wish to do outer rune work with:

- your vehicles

- your home

- computers

- heirlooms

- anything expensive and important to you

Have a set of carved runes handy. This set should be loaded for general use; that is, the carved staves should be loaded with the understandings of the runes given in chapter 3. These runes should have generic, unmodified natures, so they will serve you in many different situations and on many different objects. (See chapter 5 for how to create and load a set of carved rune staves.)

Now, pull out the specific runes that you want to work with and identify one. A very common runic trait that people often choose to affect is an object's Isa (I). Accentuating the Isa prevents the object from moving and helps prevent its theft or loss. Another useful rune is Laguz (Γ). This one will help promote the flow in an object. It may be useful for clogged gas lines in a car, plugged drains, or slow traffic. All of these things represent a flow that can be hindered or freed. Once the object's Laguz is discovered and tapped into, it can be boosted. Simply share your energy with it or draw universal energy into it.

In addition to the main rune, you may choose a modifier rune. This modifier would add to the overall effect. For example, to affect the flow of gas in a car, you may choose Laguz (Γ) as the main run and modify it with Raido (R). This combination would ensure that the gas flows through the gas line to help the vehicle move. A modifier rune for Isa might be Elhaz (Y). This combination would help to promote a solid protected state for an object.

Once you have identified the main rune and any modifiers, place them in a small bag. Put this bag in or on the object. Experiment with this process until you are comfortable with the runes' effect.

After you are satisfied or have become experienced with the effect, you can carve permanent runes for the object. These permanent runes can be carved onto individual pieces of wood or all together onto one piece. Each of the staves should be loaded with outer-rune meanings (see chapter 3) that you've determined are appropriate.

If you have decided that an Uruz-Laguz-Raido (ᚢᛚᚱ) combination works well for your vehicle, you can carve them as a bind rune on one piece of wood. You can build a small phrase to load this bind rune. Remember the Galdrathula exercise; you can use only the names of the runes or come up with an English phrase for them. A phrase for the Uruz-Laguz-Raido combination might be "strong flow to move the vehicle." Don't forget to say *alu* at the end.

Here are a few more examples that you may find useful:

ᚲᚤᚱ ᛗᛡ

Perthro Elhaz Raido Ehwaz Mannaz, alu.
"Fated protection of travel for the vehicle and rider(s)."

ᚲᚤᚱ ᛟᛡ ᚠᛚᚢ

Perthro Elhaz Raido Othala Mannaz Ansuz Laguz Uruz, alu.
"Fated protection manifested for home and family."

ᚢᛁᛏ

Uruz Isa Tiwaz, alu.
"The statue is strong, stable, and firmly in place."

ᚹᛚᚱ

Wunjo Laguz Raido, alu.
"The boat has easily flowing movement."

Believe it or not, this process gets even simpler. Once you have mastered how to access and modify an object's runic energy, you don't have to carve runes to modify it. Instead, you can use a simple two-part process to affect its energy. First, you need to identify and connect with the runic nature of the object. Then you reach out and enhance the object's nature with your own runic energy.

For example, if you do not want your car stolen, here is what you do:

1. Realize that the car's Isa is in the brakes, key ignition, and the door locks.

2. Feel the Isa energy of the car.

3. Take a deep breath and draw in universal energy.

4. Point your finger toward the car. As you exhale, let your Isa energy flow through your arm and out your finger.

5. Draw the Isa rune in the air over your car as you quietly sing the name *Isa*.

The probability that your car will be stolen has now dramatically dropped. The more often you do this process, the more the Isa nature builds up and protects your car. There is a caveat: if there is something within your karmic system that needs for you to have your vehicle stolen, this runic process will not prevent that from happening.

You may do this process to protect your home. Simply draw an Isa (|) or Elhaz (Y) on the doors and windows. To help a car get started, you may find Sowilo (⌁), Inguz (◇), Dagaz (⋈), or even Laguz (⌐) applied to the car in this manner may give it the necessary push to get going. A stoplight sometimes will respond to Dagaz (⋈). All you have to do is reach out and touch the runes that exist in the world around you, and things will start to change.

Using Inner Runes

You have also come to understand that the inner runes exist within you, and you can tap into, enhance, or modify your own runic energy. Just as you changed the energies of objects in your You level of reality, you can also modify your energy within. In fact, the energy in your "you" reality is even easier to change, because it is already your energy. You are not just in contact with it, but also you are that energy. This is not an energy you need to create or foster. This energy is the very nature of your soul.

With exercise 4, "Your Inner Futhark," you identified the various aspects of your soul that are runic in nature. Unlike inanimate objects, you do not have to reach out to touch this energy. All you need to do is enhance the energy from within.

This process is very similar to the steps taken for using outer runes. The first thing to do is create a new set of runes loaded with your specific you-level energy. When affecting objects in the outside world, you want to have a general-purpose rune set. To affect the runes in your inner world, you will want to have a set of runes specially loaded for this purpose.

This set of runes can be just the same as any other set of runes. It can be precarved, or you can carve your own. There are many different sets on the market made of different types of wood or stone. All that matters is that you find a material that best suits you and your energy. If you do not resonate with the material your runes are made of, do not choose that material. Be patient and willing to take time to find the right material. Some people choose a different material for each rune in their set.

Once you have your set of runes, you need to identify them as your own. First, if you have a symbol or bind rune of your name, you can put it on the back of the rune. Next, each of your carved runes needs to be named and loaded from your list of words from exercise 4. You reduced the phrase for each of your inner runes to one to two words for just this purpose. These words are the new names of the runes as they exist within your inner universe. Load the rune staves following the procedure outlined in the "Creating Physical Runes" portion of chapter 5.

These loaded runes now serve two purposes. This new set of runes is not a reflection of your energy—it *is* your energy. They will accurately communicate your inner and spiritual workings to your conscious mind just as they did in the divination/diagnostic process described at the end of chapter 5. From that process, you will learn what energies you need to modify.

With this second technique for using your newly loaded runes, you can pull out runes, as needed, to enhance your energy for various situations. As you did with the outer-runes technique, choose a main rune—one that depicts the energy you wish to affect—and any other runes to modify that energy.

For this technique, you may want to have bags of various colors. If your runes are in a bag of a specific color, this color may work to build on the process. Here is a partial list of colors and their energetic influences:

Blue: calming, learning, communication

Yellow: awakening, opening the mind, mental workings

Green: money, fertility, growth

Purple: spiritual matters, joy, psychic abilities

Red: anger, love, vitality

Black: hiding or hindering processes

White: protection, divine connection

Once you have become familiar with the process of accessing individual runes, you can move on to working with multiple runes. Use everything you have learned about affirmations and Galdrathula to come up with a phrase that works well with your energy.

Remember, these runes you have carved and loaded are now living beings. They do not have the complexities that human beings do; they are simple beings that each has a single focus and a single purpose. Yet they are alive, and they are powerful. Thus they deserve your respect and reverence. These are runic beings that you have brought to life from a place within your being. In all aspects, they are your children. They deserve your attention and your kindness. When they have that, they will become wondrous partners in changing your life.

The final step with working with inner runes is to make instantaneous connections with them at moments when you need their energies. At any time, you may pull in a quick burst of runic energy and charge up an inner runic trait. This technique is helpful, for example, when you are in a dangerous neighborhood. Simply pull in a burst of universal energy, then, as you exhale, power up your Elhaz (ᛉ) nature. Let this rune fill and surround you completely. When you do, you will be surrounded by a bubble of protective runic energy. Just as Elhaz energy dispels the creatures of darkness, it will repel those with ill intentions for you. They will have a harder time finding and reaching you.

You can repeat this process for any rune that you need to boost. A quick burst of Ansuz will help to clear your mind. Boosting your Tiwaz may help your willpower and keep you from overeating for a moment. Shooting energy to your Uruz may help you temporarily boost your immune system.

Remember, if you are fated to experience any of these situations, you still will. All these quick shots do is improve the probability for the situation you wish to happen. Keep in mind to not overdo it. If you are sick and you spend your day pumping up your Uruz, you will crash hard. When you are sick, you need to rest. You cannot avoid the laws of physics and nature. As long as you exist in the physical world, you must abide by its laws. But working with inner runes in this way will help you to get through things a bit more smoothly.

CONCLUSION:
SUMMING IT ALL UP

If you take anything away from this book, let it be one thing: if you start living your life in a positive way, toward the way you want it to be, then it will become that way.

- Your words reflect your thoughts.

- Your thoughts are your energy.

- Your reality is made up of your thoughts, words, and energy.

Simply stated, how you think and speak is how your life is. How you live your life is how your reality is. If you change any of these small things, all of the bigger things change with it.

Changing even little things is difficult when you have negative influences around you. To counter these negative influences, you have two options. The easiest is to remove them from your life. You may need to move, change jobs, or tell someone that you no longer want them in your life. Even though it may sound easy, it may be impossible. So what can you do?

When you make changes, do it step by step. Remember that each step has a cumulative effect. What you want to do is enjoy every success you have. Once you have a victory, no matter how small or large, enjoy and embrace it. Give thanks to all the people who are in your life and have helped you reach that goal. This simple act of gratitude solidifies that victory in place. You defend the progress you made with the expression of your gratitude.

Don't forget the list of motivators you compiled while reading the introduction. Keeping this list posted is a constant reminder of why you started your transformation process in the first place. As these motivators are reinforced, you will need less and less of a push to get you going. One day, you will find yourself living the life you want. It can happen easily.

As you build success upon your successes, you will become a guiding light. If you cannot remove yourself from the darkness that surrounds you, then allow yourself to be the light. This light will shine the way for others and show them hope. Then they will realize that they too can grow and be a light for others. Do not force change on others. Be the change you want for others by simply changing yourself. Either they will change to match your energy, or you will be drawn to new and better circumstances. Either way, you are the conduit out of a life you want to change.

Hail to those who know.

Be well.

APPENDIX: A FEW CORE PRACTICES AT A GLANCE

Meditation

In chapter 2, I introduced a rune meditation practice. Here is a summary of that practice, so you may refer back to it easily:

1. Study and memorize the properties of one to three runes that you will be exploring.

2. Set sacred space by lighting a candle and possibly incense. Calm music may even be helpful.

3. Allow yourself to be in a comfortable position—lying down or sitting.

4. Take three deep breaths in your own way, at your own pace.

5. Focus your attention on your breathing. Remember to breathe from the belly. Inhale to the count of five, exhale to the count of ten.

6. Give your conscious mind permission to rest. Reassure it that it is important and that when you are done you will be in a better place and state to work with whatever it needs.

7. Focus your thoughts on a rune.

   a. Breathe in and state the name of the rune three times.
   b. Focus on the shape of the rune and allow this shape to become bigger and surround you completely.

8. Start noticing anything that comes up on this rune.

   a. Notice any colors, textures, feelings, smells, or sounds.
   b. Try to notice if any visual images come, or thoughts, or words.
   c. Ask yourself what one word or phrase best describes this rune.

9. When you have gathered your information, open your eyes and write down your observations.

10. Go back to your relaxed position, and take three deep breaths. You will easily return to the same deep state of awareness, ready to explore the next rune.

11. Repeat steps 7 through 10 for each rune.

12. When you are done,

   a. take a few deep breaths from your chest.
   b. open your eyes.
   c. reaffirm to your conscious mind you are ready to work with it again.

Remember to log your observations. Take this in two steps. Start with your subconscious observations, then your conscious. There are no wrong answers as this is your own explanation of the runes. This is used for you to come into focus with the basic energy of the runes. It is important to note that these really are two different processes.

Rune Loading

In chapter 5, we went through the rune-loading process. Here it is again:

1. Clear your space by lighting candles and incense and doing the hammer clearing.

2. Invoke deities: State the name of gods and goddesses and invite them to help you with your work.

3. Set up working space: Lay out your runes, set up your staining materials.

4. Use the alu process of loading runes.

    a. *A.* Inhale neutral energy, exhale, intone the rune's name to tune the energy within.
    b. *L.* Inhale to gather the energy to send to the rune, exhale, intone the rune's name, and let the energy flow into the rune. As you exhale, paint the stain upon the stave. This stage may be repeated.
    c. *U.* Inhale to pull your self away from the rune and stave, exhale, intone the rune's name again to bring the rune alive in its new body.
    d. Gather any remaining energy in an inhale; as you exhale, push it out through your feet into the earth.

5. Repeat the alu process for the next few runes.
6. Gather your runes into a bag or box for safe keeping.

Clear the energies and space, if you wish.

BIBLIOGRAPHY

Antonsen, Elmer H. *Runes and German Linguistics*. New York: Mouton de Gruyter, 2002.

Ashley-Farrand, Thomas. *Mantra Sacred Words of Power* (audio book). Lafayette, CO: Sounds True, 2004.

Aswynn, Freya. *Northern Mysteries and Magick*. St. Paul, MN: Llewellyn, 1990.

Bauschatz, Pauls C. *The Well and the Tree*. Amherst: University of Massachusetts Press, 1982.

Chisholm, James Allen. *The Eddas: The Keys to the Mysteries of the North*. This can be found at *www.woodharrow.com/images/ChisholmEdda.pdf*. Originally published by Illuminati Books, 2005.

Chopra, Deepak. *Sacred Verses, Healing Sounds: The Bhagavad Gita* (audio book). Novato, CA: New World Library, 2004.

Cleasby, Richard, and Gudbrand Vigfussun. *Icelandic-English Dictionary of Old Icelandic*. Oxford: Clarendon Press, 1957.

Dickins, Bruce. *Runic and Heroic Poems of the Old Teutonic Peoples*. Cambridge: Cambridge University Press, 1915.

Ellis-Davidson, H. R. *The Road to Hel*. Cambridge, U.K.: Cambridge University Press, 1943.

———. *Gods and Myths of Northern Europe*. London: Penguin, 1964.

———. *Myths and Symbols of Pagan Europe*. Syracuse, NY: Syracuse University Press, 1988.

———. *The Lost Beliefs of Northern Europe*. London: Routledge, 1993.

Flowers, Stephen. *The Galdrabok: An Icelandic Grimoire*. York Beach, ME: Samuel Weiser, 1989.

Fries, Jan. *Helrunar: A Manual of Rune Magic*. Oxford, U.K.: Mandrake of Oxford, 1993.

Grant, Zoilita, and Neil Rohr. *The Self Healing Book*. Longmont, CO: Master Key, 1997.

Gundarson, Kveldulf. *Teutonic Magic*. St. Paul, MN: Llewellyn, 1990.

———. *Teutonic Religion*. St. Paul, MN: Llewellyn, 1993.

Handford, S. A. *The Agricola and Germania*. Translated by H. Mattingly. London: Penguin, 1970.

Haywood, John. *Historical Atlas of the Vikings*. London: Penguin, 1995.

Hollander, Lee M., trans. *The Poetic Edda*. Austin: University of Texas Press, 1986.

Looijenga, Tinke. *Texts & Contexts of the Oldest Runic Inscriptions*. Amsterdam: Brill Academic Publishers, 2003.

Page, R. I. *Runes: Reading the Past*. Berkeley: University of California Press, 1987.

Palsson, Herman, and Paul Edwards, trans. *Egil's Saga*. London: Penguin, 1976.

———. *Seven Viking Romances*. London: Penguin, 1985.

Paxson, Diana. *Taking up the Runes*. San Francisco: Weiser Books, 2005.

Pennick, Nigel. *Magical Alphabets*. York Beach, ME: Samuel Weiser, 1992.

Pennick, Nigel, and Prudence Jones. *A History of Pagan Europe*. London: Routledge, 1997.

Pert, Candace. *Molecules of Emotion: The Science Behind Mind-Body Medicine*. New York: Scribner, 1997.

Sturluson, Snorri. *The Prose Edda: Tales from Norse Mythology* . Translated by Jean Young. Berkeley: University of California Press, 1964.

———. *Heimskringla*. New York: Dover Publications, 1990.

Thorsson, Edred. *Futhark A Handbook of Rune Magic*. York Beach, ME: Samuel Weiser, 1984.

———. *Runelore*. York Beach, ME: Samuel Weiser, 1987.

———. *Nine Doors of Midgard*. St. Paul, MN: Llewellyn, 1991.

———. *Northern Magic: Rune Mysteries & Shamanism*. St. Paul, MN: Llewellyn, 1998.

Titchenell, Elsa-Brita. *The Masks of Odin: Wisdom of the Ancient Norse*. Pasadena, CA: Theosophical University Press, 1985.

Various translators. *The Sagas of Icelanders*. London: Penguin, 1997.

Willis, Tony. *The Runic Workbook*. London: Aquarius Press, 1980.

Zoega, Geir. *A Concise Dictionary of Old Icelandic*. New York: Dover Publications, 2004.

About the Author

Kaedrich Olsen has studied the runes and Northern mysteries for over 20 years. He also studied spiritually based Hypnotherapy and Shamanism in order to become a Transpersonal Hypnotherapist. Within this practice, he applied runic wisdom to develop powerful techniques his clients use to transform their lives. Kaedrich lives in Boulder, Colorado, with his wife and two daughters, where he is an accomplished leader in the Nordic spiritual community. He regularly leads ceremonies, public workshops, and lectures.

To Our Readers

Weiser Books, an imprint of Red Wheel/Weiser, publishes books across the entire spectrum of occult and esoteric subjects. Our mission is to publish quality books that will make a difference in people's lives without advocating any one particular path or field of study. We value the integrity, originality, and depth of knowledge of our authors.

Our readers are our most important resource, and we appreciate your input, suggestions, and ideas about what you would like to see published. Please feel free to contact us, to request our latest book catalog, or to be added to our mailing list.

Red Wheel/Weiser, LLC
500 Third Street, Suite 230
San Francisco, CA 94107
www.redwheelweiser.com